THROUGH THE LENS OF A MONSTER

A SERIAL KILLER ON DEATH ROW, AN UNSOLVED MURDER LIST, AND AN INMATE'S DEADLY PLAY FOR REDEMPTION

WILLIAM A. NOGUERA

SANDRA JONAS
PUBLISHING

Sandra Jonas Publishing House
PO Box 20892
Boulder, CO 80308
sandrajonaspublishing.com

Printed in the United States of America
31 30 29 28 27 26 25   1 2 3 4 5 6 7 8

Book and cover design by Sandra Jonas

Publisher's Cataloging-in-Publication Data
Names: Noguera, William A., 1964–, author.
Title: Through the Lens of a Monster: A Serial Killer on Death Row, an
    Unsolved Murder List, and an Inmate's Deadly Play for Redemption /
    William A. Noguera.
Description: Boulder, CO : Sandra Jonas Publishing, 2025.
Identifiers: ISBN 978195861022 (hardcover) | 9781954861909 (trade
    paperback) | 9781954861077 (epub) | LCCN 2025943051
Subjects: LCSH: Naso, Joseph. | Serial murderers — United States —
    Psychology. | Death row inmates — California. | Serial murders. |
    LCGFT: True crime stories. | BISAC: TRUE CRIME / Murder / Serial
    Killers.
Classification: LCC HV6248.N37 2025 | DDC 364.15232
LC record available at http://lccn.loc.gov/2025943051

Photography credits: Joseph Naso: 1, 14, 16, 17, 18, 78, 90, 150; Google Map data @2025, 210 (left); Professional Photographer magazine: 108; law enforcement: 51, 159, 168–171, 175, 196, 206, 209, 211, 214; Ken Mains: 210 (right), 213; all remaining photographs from the author's private collection.

To the victims of Joseph Naso

Contents

Author's Note

The following accounts come directly from a convicted serial killer as he revealed them to me personally. The accuracy of each story rests squarely with the man telling it.

I have checked his dates, times, and locations, and cross-checked the details to weed out any exaggerations. These chilling confessions, intertwined with his raw emotions, provide a haunting window into the twisted mind of an evil, remorseless killer.

Over the years, whenever Joseph Naso revisited a story, the core never shifted. That consistency convinced me I wasn't hearing invention, but memory. This book takes readers inside those moments, as I lived them, while staying true to the facts.

CONTENT WARNING: The following pages contain sensitive material that some readers may find disturbing, including descriptions of violence, sexual assault, and mental illness. Reader discretion is advised.

PART ONE

THE SERIAL KILLER

Joseph Naso, 2022. Age eighty-eight.

1

Arrival

When he came out to the prison yard early that first morning, I was struck by how forgettable he looked. Short and bald, he shuffled along like any old tired man trying to make it through the day. No one would have guessed what he had done. But I knew. I'd been expecting him. He had just been sentenced to death. And here he was at San Quentin: quiet, sunlit, unremarkable.

His case had been all over the local San Francisco news. Anchors called him a monster. He'd raped, strangled, and discarded six women between the 1970s and '90s. The authorities suspected there were more, but they couldn't prove it. At seventy-nine, he was the oldest man to receive the death penalty.

I held a grim distinction of my own. Decades earlier, I'd been the youngest. I was just eighteen when I committed my crime in April 1983. By the time he arrived in 2013, I had already spent twenty-five years on death row.

On that chilly November morning, he didn't waste any time. Moving slowly but deliberately, he made his way over to me.

"Why are *you* here?" he asked, squinting up at me suspiciously. "You don't look old. Or sick."

He was right. I didn't belong—at least not at first glance.

"I was assigned here by the warden," I told him. "I'm the IDAP worker. I help anyone on this yard who needs assistance."

He gave a small, knowing smile. "Huh. That so?" Then he nodded and moved on, without offering his name or asking for mine.

The ADA yard, short for American Disabilities Act, was unlike the others. Wedged between yard six (general population) and yard four (protective custody), this space was designated for older inmates and those with medical issues. Most were well over sixty, some in wheelchairs, others leaning on canes.

Mixed among them were serial killers.

And now, Joseph Naso was one of them.

As the other inmates filtered onto the yard, I tracked his slow circuit along the perimeter, his expression unreadable, his lips moving in some private conversation. A few minutes later, he looped back and stopped in front of me again.

"So if I need something, you'll help me get it?" he asked, his tone casual, but I could see the wheels turning behind his eyes.

"That's not what I said, Mr. Naso. I'm here if you need my help—walking, standing up, putting on your clothes, exercising. That sort of thing."

He cocked his head, studying me. "Call me Joe," he said. "You get paid for this?"

"Yes. It's my job."

"How much?"

I ignored his question. "What can I help you with, Joe?"

He smiled, all charm and calculation. "Coffee and something to eat. Something sweet. Only a few things. I figure a guy like you can make that happen."

I gave him my best wolfish grin, more teeth than warmth. "Are you hustling me, Mr. Naso?"

He blinked, feigning offense. "No, no, not at all," he said quickly. "Just thought you might want to help me out." He leaned in closer. "Call me Joe. You know, friends always call each other by their first names."

I nodded. "Fair enough, Joe. I'll see what I can do. No promises."

"Oh, that's great," he said, relief in his voice.

He shuffled off, his hands behind his back, like he had just closed a deal. I stood there, shaking my head. We'd barely spoken, and already he was trying to see how much he could get from me.

When the wheelchairs finally rolled up to the entrance, I walked over as the gate buzzed open.

I nodded to the first man waiting—Gary Hines, his blue eyes sharp beneath a flat-top that hadn't changed in years. "Morning, Mr. Hines. How're you holding up today?"

"Not bad, Bill." He smiled, the creases in his face deepening.

The yard release area was narrow, designed for a single inmate on foot, not for one in a wheelchair, much less a long line of them. After watching him angle back and forth a few times, I stepped in.

"Hang tight," I said. "Let me do it my way."

Before he could respond, I gripped the chair by its frame, lifted him free of the bottleneck, and carried him into the yard. I set him down gently, pushed him where he wanted to go, and locked the brake.

"Appreciate it," he said, zipping up his jacket.

One by one, I brought in the rest—some asked for help and others managed on their own. When the last of the seventy or so men were inside the yard and the gate locked behind us, the officers disappeared back into East Block.

As I made my way back to where I'd locked Hines in place, I could feel the eyes on me, measuring and suspicious. Even though I'd been working on the yard a couple of weeks, some of the men were still afraid of me.

I didn't blame them.

When I first landed on death row in 1988, there was only one yard. But years of murders, rapes, and extortion forced the administration to divide us into smaller, more manageable groups, separated by chain-link fences. These new yards were created not just for control, but for survival.

I came from general population, where violence is currency and I'd learned how to spend it wisely. Now I was placed among inmates removed for their own safety. To them, I wasn't a caregiver. I was a threat.

The serial killers, rapists, and pedophiles feared me most—and with good reason. They're reviled by everyone. In the prison hierarchy, they're at the bottom. Even professional hitmen—those who kill for money or business—get more respect. But those who kill for pleasure or prey on the vulnerable are seen as perverse and disposable. Vermin.

The rules are clear: If you're in close proximity to one of these predators, you take him out. No questions. No mercy. Otherwise, *you* become the target.

That's why men like Naso ended up here, in the ADA yard.

But I didn't want any of these old, broken men to fear me. That felt abusive and wrong. The warden had trusted me with this assignment, and I wasn't about to let him down.

Still, the job came with risks. The convict code runs deep. In the eyes of some, working in protective custody—especially without killing one of the predators—wasn't just crossing a line. It was betrayal. And being the only man assigned to two yards only painted a bigger target on my back. On my days off from the ADA yard, I returned to general population, where gangs ran deep and weapons were hidden in shadows.

I'd chosen not to follow the code.

And in prison, that choice could get me killed.

The men settled into their routines: card games at the steel tables, slow laps around the cement, quiet conversations in corners. Naso stood alone, back to the brick wall, watching everything.

I turned to Hines. "Where'd you like to go?"

"If you don't mind, push me over to the sink? I need some hot water for my coffee."

"Not a problem." I grabbed the handles and started toward the front corner.

As we rolled along, he shifted in his seat to look back at me. "So, Bill, how do you like it out here?" he asked with a grin. "Happy I got you this gig?"

"Absolutely."

He hadn't just recommended me for the job. He'd filed a lawsuit, won, and then told the administration he needed an IDAP worker. He made sure it was me.

Hines was a known jailhouse lawyer, spending most of his time in the law library, filing suits against the California Department of Corrections and Rehabilitation for every violation he could find. Hell, he'd made a career of it.

The CDCR hated convicts like him. While most jailhouse lawyers were just blowing smoke, Hines actually won cases—some for himself, others for inmates he helped. That made him dangerous. The prison fought back with the same rulebook, making his time as miserable as possible. For Hines, it became a game of cat and mouse, and a reason to live.

It hadn't always been that way. Twenty-five years earlier, he'd been on yard one, general population, lifting weights near where I worked out. But he couldn't keep his mouth shut, and eventually that got him into trouble. After assaulting a few guys, he ended up in the Adjustment Center—the hole—where the worst of the worst go. That's when it hit him: he was in the big leagues, and he'd just struck out.

From there, it was a straight shot to protective custody. Then fate, or maybe karma, dealt a blow. Parkinson's took his legs. Now he couldn't walk, and plenty of men wanted him dead.

But I liked the guy. He told stories with flair, exaggerated everything, and kept things interesting. So when he asked me if I'd be willing to take the IDAP position, I said yes, even though it could make me a marked man back in general population.

At the sink, Hines filled his mug with hot water and dumped in a scoop of instant coffee. "This yard's nothing like yours," he said. "Wall-to-wall weirdos. See that guy with the hat at that table?" He nodded to the right, and I followed his gaze.

"Uh-huh," I said.

"That sick fuck killed over twenty girls. Chopped them up, put the meat in chili, and served it to cops at a picnic."

I stared at him. "C'mon. He didn't really—"

"I'm serious. They call him the Chili King. Every guy at that table? Serial killer. They play cards together and trade pictures of their victims. Like baseball cards."

He gestured again. "The guy to his right? That's the Trailside Killer. The other two—I forget their nicknames, but they're just as bad."

I crouched beside his wheelchair. "What's the deal with the pictures? Why trade them?"

"They've got a club," he said flatly.

I raised an eyebrow.

"They pair off, huddle in the back of the yard, and compare stories. Most guys don't even know the club exists, but I pay attention. I was on yard four with some of them."

He paused, his tone darker now. "Bonin was in it, before they executed him. Kraft. Ramirez. Ng. I've even heard rumors about guys in other states, maybe even on the street. Makes you wonder."

I nodded, keeping my expression neutral.

I knew a lot more than I let on. The man in the hat was Bill Lester Suff. Beside him, David Carpenter, the Trailside Killer. I'd talked to them both. I already knew about the club. And the cards.

But I also knew the value of listening. Hines had a way of stitching together rumors and half-truths that often revealed more than he realized.

I scanned the yard. When I first arrived on death row, I studied the men I feared most—murderers, shot-callers, lifers with something to prove. That was survival.

But serial killers unsettled me in a different way. It wasn't just what they had done. It was the calm that followed, the way they moved through the world untouched by the weight of their crimes.

My ability to read people had started long before prison. My father ruled with violence, and I learned to anticipate every change in tone, every twitch of muscle. That vigilance followed me to death row. It had kept me alive.

I glanced back at the table. They sat comfortably, laughing and holding court like retired businessmen swapping stories.

What passed between them? Recognition? Admiration? Or just the comfort of knowing they weren't alone?

I didn't say a word, but something stirred inside me.

A quiet idea. Not new, exactly, just sharper.

Shortly after noon, it was our turn to head back in. From the ADA yard, you could see the others cycling through. Everyone watched. You always knew when your time was coming.

We left in reverse order, wheelchairs first. As I maneuvered Hines into the vestibule, a voice behind me cut through the noise—cocky, eager to impress.

"I'm a professional photographer," the man said. "Been published in magazines. Real ones. My outdoor work's what I'm known for."

I glanced over my shoulder. Naso stood near the gate, talking to Suff.

"Oh, yeah?" Suff said. "I'm no photographer, but I used to make a mean pot of chili. Cops lined up for it. I even won an award."

He changed the story a little every time, but the delivery remained the same: somewhere between a joke and a confession. With him, you could never be sure.

They both looked my way.

"Bill. Joe," I said, giving them a short nod. "See you tomorrow."

Suff gave a lazy wave.

Naso took a step forward. "You'll get me the things I asked for, right? Like we agreed?"

I didn't answer. I just turned and pushed Hines through to the other side.

2

The Envelope

The next morning, I packed for work in the cell I'd lived in for decades, barely 4.5 by 9.5 feet. A towel, tumbler, socks, jacket, and beanie. For lunch, I tossed in a pouch of mackerel, a peanut butter sandwich, and a small bag of chips.

The first of December was coming up—time to shop at the canteen. When I was first sentenced to death row, I imagined a cot, four bare walls, and years of tasteless food and bleak silence. I was wrong. We had TVs, stereos, and even phone privileges. Once a month, we could buy snacks and supplies. My artwork paid for it all.

I measured out a few scoops of Taster's Choice into a Ziploc and tucked in a couple of candy bars.

For Joseph Naso.

He'd been on my mind the moment I woke up. Who was he, really? Beneath the bland exterior, what kind of man could commit those crimes?

The day before, something in me had shifted. I felt a pull I could no longer ignore.

I'd been around serial killers for years, passing them on other yards and talking to them through fences. But this was different. Now I had sustained, daily access. I could study them up close, unnoticed. And I could write it all down.

The outside world had no idea what they were like. But if people saw what I saw—if they heard what I heard—maybe they'd finally understand the true nature of the monsters walking among us.

As the IDAP worker, I was always the first one out, usually a little after 7:00. That early hour mattered. The yard was mine alone—time to push my body, clear my head, and steel myself before the others arrived. I needed that ritual, especially that day, because I was about to take the first real step in my plan: to befriend the serial killers on the ADA yard and earn their trust.

I'd gone over it again and again in my mind. The key was to get close enough that they'd lower their guard and start revealing the parts of themselves they usually kept hidden. I didn't need to be one of them. I just needed them to believe I was.

My strategy hinged on something universal, something all of us crave, even in prison—especially in prison. Attention. And beneath that, something deeper: affirmation. Maybe even respect.

But I wouldn't give those things freely. Sometimes, withholding attention yielded more than offering it, and I planned to use that to my advantage.

Like every yard, this one had a basketball half-court at one end. At the other, near the back wall, stood pull-up bars, dip bars, and a heavy bag that had hung untouched until I got there.

I filled my tumbler at the sink, stretched, and started my workout: eight three-minute rounds on the heavy bag. Each round, I hit harder and faster, my strikes echoing across the yard. Then I ran two miles around the perimeter, followed by five hundred push-ups, pull-ups, squats, and dips.

In prison, strength keeps the real predators at bay. That's why I was still alive. At forty-nine, I was a man to be respected, giving me a measure of safety.

Shortly after 8 a.m., the ADA inmates began to arrive. One by one, cuffed behind their backs, they entered through the gate. The officer uncuffed them and let them loose.

Naso was fourth in line. The instant he stepped into the yard, he waved me over, but I raised my finger, signaling him to wait. He dropped his things on one of the steel card tables and tugged on his jacket and beanie, never taking his eyes off me.

He looked like he had something to say, but I kept him waiting. If he sensed that I didn't see him as important, he might try harder to get my attention, giving me the edge I needed.

After getting everyone settled and setting Hines up at the pinochle table with his coffee, I walked over to the pull-up bars to gather my things for a shower. Within seconds, Naso was at my side, jittery with impatience.

"Did you forget me?" he asked. "I've been waiting to talk, but you're all over the place helping everybody else."

He gave off a rank, musty odor, thick and lingering.

"Mr. Naso," I said evenly, "helping the other men on this yard *is* my job. That's why I'm out here. Is there something you need?"

"Joe," he said quickly. "Please call me Joe. I just thought, you know, maybe we could talk. We have a lot in common."

"We do?"

"Yes, yes. I asked around. You're an artist. You've been in magazines. Everyone knows who you are." He glanced toward the table where he'd left his things. "Wait here. I have something to show you."

Naso returned with a large manila envelope. "Let's go over there," he said, leading me to the farthest table from the rest.

Sitting down, he motioned for me to do the same. "I'd like your opinion," he blurted out. "I've brought some photographs for you to look at. Tell me what you think."

He handed me the envelope. I didn't know what to expect, but the intensity of his eyes said he needed something from me—validation maybe or approval.

Exactly what I'd hoped for.

I opened the envelope slowly. He gripped the table, tight with anticipation. When I finally slid the pictures out, he exhaled and relaxed, as if he had been holding his breath.

Still, I said nothing. I just gave him the empty envelope and focused on the eight-by-tens in front of me.

The first showed a young girl from the sixties or early seventies, judging by her clothes. She smiled brightly into the camera, almost too brightly, like she was trying to please the photographer.

This second was a portrait of a woman in her mid-twenties. Blond, blue eyes, too much makeup. There was something sad and vulnerable about her expression. My gut tightened. Was she still alive? Or was she one of Joe Naso's victims?

I moved on to the third photo, a black-and-white landscape shot of a pond. That's when I saw his talent. The image had mood and texture, capturing a haunting loneliness.

The rest were similar, portraits and landscapes, carefully composed—the work of a man who had spent years mastering his craft.

Then I reached the last two.

One was a photo of a younger Joe, holding his camera and smiling with easy confidence.

"It's a good shot," he said, smirking.

"It is. They're all impressive. I didn't realize you had this kind of talent."

"*Skill.* Talent's overrated. What I have is skill—perfected over years. Like a surgeon. I leave only what's necessary."

He leaned in and pointed at the photos I still held, his fingernails rimmed with black grime. "You missed one."

I shuffled the stack and froze.

It was a collage. The younger Naso again in the center, surrounded by several smaller photos of women, arranged like a collection.

His trophies. What had become of them?

In the center, he had signed it to me:

Best wishes to Bill N.
Joe Naso

A chill ran down my spine.

Collage from Naso. 1970s.

"I thought you might like an autographed gift," he said.

I forced myself to meet his gaze. "Thank you. Your work is . . . powerful."

"I knew you'd appreciate it."

I took a chance. "Joe, where are these women? Are they still alive?"

He held my gaze for a long moment, and then he smiled and tapped his temple with one finger. "They're alive in here."

A weight settled in my gut, but I didn't press him. Not yet. He wasn't ready. He wanted to be seen as an artist, as someone worthy of respect. And that meant he'd come back.

"I almost forgot," I said. "I brought you something."

His face lit up. "You remembered?"

"Give me a second." I walked over to my things, and when I returned, Naso had put away the photographs, except the one he'd signed for me.

I set a paper bag on the table. "Here's what you wanted."

He rubbed his hands, almost giddy, and pulled out the coffee and candy bars, inspecting each item like it was a rare treasure. "Gee, thanks."

"Enjoy them, Joe. And thank you for the gift." I turned to leave.

"Hey, wait—where're you going?"

"I've got to see someone. I'll bring you samples of my work sometime. Maybe you could give me *your* opinion."

His eyes widened in surprise. "Oh, okay, Bill."

I crossed the yard, a spark of excitement rising in my chest. A part of me recoiled at the exchange, but another part was energized by the opening it created.

I'd made contact.

And just maybe, Joe Naso was going to talk.

Joseph Naso photography.

Joseph Naso. 1970s.

3

The Approach

On a cool morning in May, six months into the job, I rose at 5 a.m. as usual. After washing up at the tiny sink, I sat on my five-gallon bucket and used the bunk frame as a writing desk. The news murmured from the TV as I spread out my pages of notes.

Sipping my barely tolerable Taster's Choice coffee, I reviewed the previous day's entry and mapped out my next moves—who to approach and what to say. This had become my routine now: study the men during yard time and then rush back to record the details before they faded. The patterns were beginning to emerge: small tells, habits, obsessions.

Of all the killers, I was getting the closest to Naso, slowly and deliberately, on my terms. We spoke nearly every day, mostly about art. As soon as he entered the yard, he'd seek me out, anxious to share his photographs and get my opinion.

I kept trying new angles to build trust and deepen the connection. Some days, I steered the conversation toward his gear—cameras, lenses, film stock—until he lost himself in talk of his craft and let personal details slip. Other days, I'd pivot to football or baseball. He never missed a sports headline.

Now and then, I made excuses not to talk, just to leave him hungry for the interaction. The goal was to keep him off-balance, isolated, though he was already doing a good job of that himself. His nonstop

One of the many photographs of Naso and "his girls." 1970s.

bragging about his photography career had already alienated most of the men on the yard. He thought he was better than everyone else. That made me, by design, his only friend.

The sound of breakfast trays echoed down the tier. That morning, it was two boiled eggs in the shell, a banana, and a pear. I'd eat that. But I never touched anything that was prepared and left exposed. Too many guys in the kitchen hated serial killers, rapists, and pedophiles. You couldn't trust what they'd slip into the food. If waffles had shown up, I would have skipped the tray and made the oatmeal I bought from the canteen.

Flipping through my notes, I thought again about the book I'd started sketching in my mind about Naso and the other serial killers I'd gotten to know. The yard had its share of high-profile predators: Bill Suff and David Carpenter, sure, but also Randy Kraft, the "Score-card Killer," who lived next door, and Martin Kipp—"Dr. Crazy"—my neighbor on the other side.

Naso stood out among them as the easiest to talk to. And he kept records. That compulsion to document his crimes ultimately led to his arrest decades after the murders. According to news reports, he had a long history of lesser offenses—petty theft and grand larceny—but it was an April 2010 parole check at his home in Reno that set everything in motion.

The officers uncovered a trove of material: photographs of partially nude women who appeared dead or unconscious, along with a journal describing rapes of underage girls and women stretching back to the 1950s. And then came the most damning find—a single sheet of lined paper tucked in a notebook on his kitchen table, easy to miss among the clutter.

On it, in Joe's unmistakable scrawl, were ten entries: "Girl near Heldsburg [sic] Mendocino Co." . . . "Girl on Mt. Tam." No names. No dates. Just locations. Investigators quickly suspected what the list really was—a roll call of murder victims.

At his trial, Naso represented himself, insisting on his innocence. Investigators presented the discoveries from his home alongside DNA evidence to convict him of four murders: Roxene Roggasch, Carmen Colon, Pamela Parsons, and Tracy Tafoya. During the penalty phase, they tied him to two more—Sharieea Patton and Sara Dylan. It was enough for the jury to give him the death penalty.

The more I spoke with him, the more I found myself needing to know—not just about the other four murders, but about what his victims had suffered in their final moments. I wanted to offer something to the families, whether the cases were officially closed or not. They deserved to know how their loved ones died. They deserved some measure of closure.

That morning, my agenda was clear: show Joe a glimpse of my work and the recognition it had earned. I'd dangled the idea for weeks, knowing anticipation would make the payoff stronger. Now it was time to give him just enough to keep him hooked—and to shift me from peer to someone he might admire, even envy, as an artist, a man, and, yes, a killer. More than that, he had to believe I understood him and his vision, however twisted.

If he felt both the connection he craved and the urge to impress me, he might finally start feeding me the truth.

I kept thinking about a mother I'd seen on the news years earlier, pleading through tears. Her daughter had been abducted and murdered.

"Can someone please tell me what happened to my child?"

Her words had stayed with me, planting something I hadn't forgotten.

And now, in an unexpected twist of fate, I had a job that could help me expose the kind of killer who took lives for no other reason than the desire to do it.

I could understand murder driven by rage, revenge, even money. There was no excuse for it, but I could grasp it. I thought often about my own crime, about the red-hot fury that had driven me to kill my girlfriend's mother, who had forced her to abort our child. Not a day passed that I didn't wish I could go back and stop that young man.

But this hunger to kill for pleasure was something else entirely. Something darker. Something we could barely fathom.

Still, I wanted to try.

‑‑‑‑‑

Shortly after 7 a.m., the loudspeaker crackled to life with the usual announcement: "Yard release, yard release. All inmates going to yard, turn on your lights, roll back your mattress, and have the items you're taking outside ready for inspection."

Minutes later, I heard my name. "Noguera, get prepared." I had ten minutes.

I turned off the TV and sat still, focusing on my breath, calming my mind while sharpening my senses. I entered a heightened state, attuned to every sound and scent. In prison, reading the energy of a place could mean the difference between life and death. I did this every time before stepping outside.

I made it my business to know everyone's routines. When they changed, violence often followed. If I sensed a shift—agitation, silence, eyes darting—I knew something was off. That awareness kept me alive.

In the yard vestibule, I'd be cuffed briefly. A sitting duck in a cage. Anything could happen—a ceramic knife, a rolled-up newspaper used like a spear. I had to stay alert.

I packed my nylon bag quickly, double-checking that my portfolio and folder of press clippings were well concealed. I also hid my notes around the cell. Just a week earlier, officers had confiscated a batch during a random search, and I'd had to recreate them from memory. It wouldn't be the last time.

Normally, my tier officer strip-searched me and went through every item I carried. But since I had accepted the IDAP job, the process had relaxed. That morning, he just nodded and said "Get ready," before launching into small talk about politics.

Still, I had to make it past the scan machine near the yard door. I headed down the fourth tier and descended the stairs.

"*Buenos días*, Noguera," the gun-rail officer on the third floor called down. "On your way to the nursing home, I see." He chuckled.

I shrugged. "It's a job, boss."

On the first floor, I approached the scan machine. The yard sergeant stood nearby.

"Morning, Sergeant, what's the word?"

"Thunderbird."

"What's the price?"

"Forty, twice." He smiled. "On your way to where the serial killers go to rest?"

"Something like that. You never know, I might learn something."

He snorted. "Those creeps don't have a thing I want to learn. Every time one of them walks by, I picture what they've done, and it fucks with my head."

He wasn't wrong. They'd all committed unimaginable acts—someone's worst nightmare made real. But I had a plan, and I wasn't about to stop now.

When I stepped through the East Block door, the air was cool but not cold. Still, after decades in the Bay Area, I knew gray clouds could turn into rain without warning. That worked to my advantage. Rain gear and a jacket helped me hide what I'd brought for Joe.

During my workout, I rehearsed the approach in my head. Every word had to carry weight, every detail had to sound natural. With Naso, one wrong move could turn admiration into suspicion.

4

The Portfolio

I was waiting at the yard gate when the first man stepped through. Suff, cane in hand, limped past me.

"Morning, Bill," he said with a nod.

"How's it going today?" I said, falling into step beside him.

He paused mid-shuffle. "When you have a second, I have something to show you." Then he continued his halting walk toward one of the steel benches at the back of the yard, trailed by his sidekick, Ward Weaver.

Everyone knew what Suff was—his history wasn't a secret. But what intrigued me was how he moved through this place like a man running a club, not serving time for murdering women. And Weaver followed closely, always just a few steps behind. Thick-set and dull-eyed, he looked like a mountain troll, clinging to Suff like a disciple.

Their dynamic was strange but deliberate. Suff gave orders. Weaver obeyed.

Still, they had mutual benefits. Weaver fancied himself a writer—churning out self-published books under the name Alex O'Neill—and Suff, never one to pass up a title, dubbed himself editor-in-chief. It was a win-win: Weaver got to play author, and Suff got to pretend he was running a publishing empire from death row. Around the prison, they were known as Mr. Peabody and Sherman: Suff the overbearing brainiac, Weaver the loyal dimwit.

But something darker was beneath it all.

I'd known about the serial killer club and trading cards, but what I saw over time was worse than I imagined. This wasn't just twisted bravado or morbid nostalgia. It was a full-blown subculture. They swapped tokens like currency, compared kills like baseball stats, and cataloged their stories with pride.

And it wasn't limited to the yard. They had fans on the outside who wrote letters, sent money, and even visited, drawn in by the perverse fascination with men who killed for pleasure.

In that world, Suff wasn't just another inmate. He was a star. His prison ID and personalized victim cards could sell for hundreds. Signed? Thousands.

He was a killer—and he knew his value.

After the last person came into the ADA yard, the gate clanged shut. I scanned the group. No sign of Joe Naso. Where the hell was he? I'd hauled everything out for nothing. If he didn't show, I'd have to smuggle it all back in.

I busied myself helping the men who needed it, my eyes drifting now and then to Suff. He was holding a yellow folder, casting glances my way, clearly waiting for a moment to corner me. I let him stew. That was part of the strategy: make them wait, make them want my attention.

About an hour later, I wandered over to the drinking fountain. Suff saw his opening and limped over, pretending to be thirsty.

"Hey, Bill, you busy? I got something to show you."

His breath hit me: boiled eggs, cabbage, and something rotten.

I tried not to inhale. "Just about done. What's up?"

"You know, I've edited several books, including Ward's highly successful series—"

I cut in. "Really? Who's his publisher?"

He paused, caught off guard. "Uh . . . his publisher is Amazon. His books have done really well."

"Man, that's impressive."

"Yes, yes, but I've written a lot myself." He opened the yellow folder. "That's what I wanted to show you."

As he fished out a manila envelope, a card slipped from the folder and fell to the ground. I bent down to pick it up—it was stiff and laminated like a sports trading card.

But it wasn't an image of an athlete. It was a nude woman, suspended in midair, her back to the camera. Her skin had been peeled back, exposing her ribs and lower back. A pair of panties had been pulled down and away.

I froze.

This was one of Suff's "collectibles."

When I glanced up, he was smirking, but his eyes were cold. He was watching me, gauging my reaction.

I handed the card back with a blank expression. "I think you dropped something."

"So I did." He giggled strangely and tucked the card back into the folder. "You gotta keep your flock in line, or you'll lose 'em."

And just like that, the predator vanished and the editor returned.

"Here you go," he said, offering the manila envelope. "One of my many manuscripts. A short story. I think you'll find it interesting."

I started to open it, bracing myself for the inevitable sales pitch. Suff was winding up when I spotted movement behind him. A security escort was nearing the yard gate, and in the wheelchair in front of them sat Joe Naso.

Finally.

The guards exchanged annoyed looks. Everyone knew Joe didn't need assistance. Sure enough, once they arrived at the gate, he stood and walked into the sally port on his own, looking smug.

I turned to Suff. "Time to earn my keep."

He started to say something, but I cut him off. "I'll read your story and let you know what I think."

As I waited for Naso, Suff kept talking. "Take your time, Bill. Actually, you can have the story. A gift. Here, let me sign it."

I almost laughed, but I caught myself. If I wanted these men to open up to me, I had to take them seriously. As sick as it was that a serial rapist and killer like Suff was treated like a minor celebrity, I had to treat him that way too.

I thanked him for the signed story and walked over to Naso standing by the open gate. When I pulled his new wheelchair through, he lowered himself into it.

"Thanks," he said.

The wheelchair was his latest manipulation, guaranteeing my full attention. I wouldn't need to finish my work before checking in with him. He'd made himself my work.

When Naso wanted something, he simply cut out all the obstacles in his way.

I gripped the handles. "Where to?"

He waved vaguely, then made a circular motion. "It's a nice day. Let's take a walk."

"Okay, Joe, but since when do you need a wheelchair? You seemed fine yesterday."

"I saw the doctor this morning and told him my legs hurt. He gave me this brand-new chair." He smiled broadly. "Nice, right?"

"It is, but do your legs actually hurt?"

"No." He laughed, pleased with himself.

We made slow laps around the yard. Suddenly, Joe called out, "Stop!"

We'd reached the far edge of the yard, near the wall that separated us from the outside world. Joe stood up, dug into his jacket pocket, and pulled out a bag of sunflower seeds. He scattered a handful across the ground.

In seconds, a dozen doves swarmed his feet.

I stepped back a few yards, watching. Naso looked peaceful, almost childlike, with a faint smile. The image transported me back to when I was a young boy feeding doves with my grandfather.

I walked over to my lunch bag, took out a pack of sunflower kernels and a slice of bread, and returned. He was still feeding the birds, deep in thought.

"Mind if I join you?" I asked.

"Not at all. They're hungry, and I'm just about out."

As we fed the doves side by side, the rest of the yard faded. We were only a few yards from the others, but the quiet, rhythmic act of feeding the birds made it feel like a world apart.

Naso seemed to feel it too. His eyes softened as he watched the birds peck at the ground, as if he'd drifted somewhere far away.

I spoke quietly, using the tone I'd practiced, the one I thought he'd respond to. "You know, it's a moment like this when I really pay attention—the way their feathers catch the light, how they move together without making a sound. Most people wouldn't notice."

I scattered another handful of seeds. "I try to take it all in—the light, the color, the emotion—and later bring it back to life through my work."

Joe scoffed, still watching the birds. "Most people look right at the world and don't see a damn thing. No imagination. No soul."

This was the opening I'd been waiting for. "You've been asking to see my work."

He nodded at me, eyebrows raised, waiting.

"I brought you some samples. Figured it was time to show you."

His face brightened. "Oh yeah?"

I walked back to my things and grabbed the portfolio and folder. I'd considered waiting until later to give them to him, but I wanted to study his reaction.

When I joined him again, he was still surrounded by birds, staring into the middle distance. I watched him a few minutes longer. Then he turned to me, his eyes locking on mine.

And there it was.

A flash behind the stillness—sharp, alert, cold. The harmless old man fell away, and in his place stood the man he'd always been. Predatory. Dangerous. I'd seen that look before. I didn't need evidence or a trial transcript to confirm what he was.

Joe Naso was a killer. A serial killer.

Like a seasoned cop who can read someone in seconds, I'd developed an instinct for seeing through a convict's mask. The eyes always told the truth. And Joe's revealed everything.

He wasn't remorseful. He wasn't reformed. He was reliving his crimes—rape, torture, murder—as if they'd happened yesterday. If he could, he'd do it all over again.

The way he lingered in that moment, so pleased with himself, made my skin crawl.

His eyes dropped to the items in my hand.

"Those for me?" he asked.

I let the silence stretch—not only to give myself a second to regroup, but to make him feel the weight of what I was sharing. "Yes," I said finally. "This is my work. My way of capturing the world so I never forget it."

But I didn't step toward him.

He needed to come to me, to see me as the one in control. If he believed I was the bigger predator, he might lower his guard, though brute dominance—the kind that threatened his ego—wouldn't work. The authority he respected had to be measured and deliberate.

But it wasn't only about power. It was also about recognition. If I valued his "art," no matter how disturbing, I became a worthy audience. Like a submissive wolf showing its throat to the alpha, Naso had to feel both dominated and safe.

That's the paradox most detectives and journalists miss.

Serial killers like Naso don't explain themselves—not to people who won't understand. They don't lay out motives or reasoning because, in their minds, it's all self-evident. Anyone with their level of intelligence and cunning should already get it.

That's why so many true crime accounts rely on speculation. The facts—trial transcripts, police reports, evidence logs—are all public record. But real insight? You don't get that from a sit-down interview. You don't get it by simply asking.

As long as a serial killer sees himself as the dominant one, the smartest in the room, he'll never share anything of real value. He knows what you want. He might even toy with you, elevating his own sense of control. But he won't give you the truth.

That was my advantage. I was one of them, with my own dark reputation. I knew how to project strength without confrontation—and how to observe closely without intruding or setting off alarms.

Now, Joe made the first move. Looking right at me, he stepped forward and put his hand out.

I waited until he was just within reach, then took a step toward him.

He instinctively lowered his eyes and stepped back.

I had him.

And best of all, he knew it.

5

The Dance

I stared into Naso's eyes, letting him feel the force of mine—hard, unblinking. Then I gave him a half smile, just enough to suggest I knew something he didn't. This was the moment I'd been rehearsing.

"Let's see what you do with this," I said, handing him the portfolio and folder. "Art has a way of showing who a man really is."

I turned to walk away.

Behind me, Joe called out, "I've never pretended. Art chose me, and I embraced her."

I didn't break stride. "We'll see, Mr. Naso. We'll see."

When I glanced back, he was clutching the items to his bony chest, as if someone might take them from him.

For the next hour, I left him alone. But I watched. He'd clap softly when he turned a page, his lips moving as he muttered to himself. Every so often, he would glance toward me, his eyes glinting.

I pretended not to notice.

He needed space to drop the act. To stop playing the part of the wrongly convicted old man and let the real Joseph Naso come to the surface. Not the man who charmed women, manipulated cops, and posed as a loving father and professional photographer. I didn't want the version he fed reporters or the courts.

I wanted the truth—the killer, the sadist, the narcissist. The man who still held the key to at least four unsolved murders.

The urgency hit me in that moment. Naso was old and frail. How long did I have before the truth died with him?

And I wasn't naive—I knew the danger was only growing.

For the past six months, I'd been moving between the ADA yard and general population. So far, no one had challenged me, though I could feel the heat of eyes tracking my every move. Ghost, the highest-ranking member of the prison gang that ruled the yard, had held the wolves off—so far. We'd come up together, survivors of the violence that forged men like us.

But that protection could vanish in a heartbeat.

And if word ever got out about this book—about my real reason for getting close to Naso—I'd be in even deeper trouble. It was bad enough, in their eyes, that I hadn't taken him out when I had the chance. That alone marked me as suspect.

But if I exposed his secrets? If I led the cops to the bodies? That would make me something worse: a snitch.

And in here, snitches don't get warnings.

Still, I kept going. Because this wasn't just about me. It wasn't even about Naso. It was about the women who never came home. And the families who still didn't know why.

With a deep breath, Joe closed the portfolio and folder. As if in a trance, he stepped into the open yard and began an eerie pantomime. He strode to a woman only he could see—reaching out, taking her hand, and pulling her into a slow, turning waltz. His arms wrapped around empty air, his feet gliding in rhythm to music only he could hear.

For several minutes, he danced with his invisible partner. Then suddenly he stopped. With a theatrical flourish, he bowed deeply to the ghost, turned, and walked back to the table with my artwork.

Sensing an opportunity, I left the fence line, quietly excusing myself from the conversation I'd been having. I followed Joe across the yard to where he was once again hunched over my portfolio, flipping pages with almost reverent attention.

I stopped a few feet away, within earshot, just in time to hear him talking under his breath. He tapped one of the plastic sleeves with a bony finger and sneered. "Whore," the slur lingering in the air.

Without a word, I sat down across from him at the stainless-steel table. We were tucked into a far corner of the yard, near a group of inmates playing cards, but with enough distance to feel apart, separated under a sky that kept shifting from sun to storm, the clouds heavy with rain.

A gust of wind kicked up, scattering some of the press clippings Joe had laid out. He scrambled to gather them, and as he did, he noticed me. His eyes widened in surprise.

"You move quietly for a big guy. Didn't even hear you sit down."

He tapped the portfolio again and offered a knowing grin. "When I heard you were an artist, I never imagined this. Not in a million years. You take pictures with your eyes."

"That's a good way to put it," I said. "My eyes are the lens. My mind, the camera."

He flipped to another page, marveling at the image. "But these . . . these are something else. I can't believe they're drawings. They look like photographs. The light, the detail—it's like you captured the moment straight from your mind."

When he talked about art, the frail old man vanished. So did the rapist, the murderer, the sadist. What remained was a different mask: the passionate artist. That was his true talent—not photography, not even murder—but deception.

And now I could see it clearly: Joseph Naso could switch between personas at will. He wore each one with conviction, fooling even a trained eye—if only for a moment.

My conversations with Joe became routine, easy and familiar. His words came more freely now, without the guarded pauses he used in the beginning.

He started dropping hints about his crimes—never much at once, just a breadcrumb here, a shadow of a confession there. A casual reference to a location. A victim's first name. A childhood memory twisted into justification. I never pushed. That wasn't my role—not yet. I kept my distance just enough to make him feel the absence and remind him that my attention had to be earned.

Some mornings, I made a show of talking to others. One day late that summer, it was Bill Suff.

When I circled back to Joe, he was visibly agitated. He didn't try to hide it.

"Why were you talking to him?" he snapped.

"I'm interested in serial killers," I said. "In their perspective."

He scoffed, bitter. "Suff's a fucking idiot. Killed for a few months and got himself caught. Amateur hour. Me? They didn't touch me for sixty years—and when they finally did, it was dumb luck. Pure chance. And they still got it wrong."

He leaned in, his voice lower now, full of pride.

"It's not rage. It's not impulse. It's an art. That's what people don't get. It's what I do. I'm a fucking artist."

He said it like he needed me to believe it.

I showed no reaction, but inside, everything clicked into place—this wasn't bravado. It was doctrine. He saw himself as a creator, not a killer. And he wanted an audience who understood that. Someone who saw the genius in the horror.

The kind of man he thought I was.

Over the next year, I gave him space to feel in control of the dialogue. Sometimes we'd go a month without touching on art at all. He'd veer off into baseball, the World Series, or the NFL, capable of rattling off stats going back decades.

I played along, always listening, always observing. The last thing I wanted was for him to sense I had an agenda.

As the weeks passed, he showed me more photos of his "girls," as he called them. He'd ask for things too: coffee, candy, whatever small luxuries I could get for him. It was part of his game, a way to test the boundaries of our connection.

When the timing felt right, I'd bring in another portfolio or slip him another article, letting him feel included and respected. It kept him talking. And the more at ease he became, the more the poison surfaced.

"Women are all the same," he'd say. "Disgusting whores. They don't know how to live. That's why they need men. You have to keep them in line."

That was Joe. He'd lure me in with talk of film grain and composition and then snap cold and cruel without warning. And I let it happen—because each moment like that brought me closer to what I needed: the truth.

Soon, he'd ask me for help. And after that, everything would change.

6

Rockhead

It was an overcast day in July 2015, and Naso and I were sitting across from each other at a steel table, flipping through one of my portfolios. He was unusually quiet.

"People say you're not to be messed with," he finally said. "That you'll hurt anyone who disrespects you—or someone you care about." He looked at me closely. "Is that true? That you'd protect someone who might need it?"

I didn't answer. Joe rarely said anything without an angle. I just listened.

He wiped his face. "We're friends, right? If you needed help, I'd do whatever I could."

I knew where this was going.

On Saturday, my day off, he'd crossed paths with Rockhead, a former gang member in his sixties who claimed to be hearing impaired. But the truth was, he had likely faked it. The doctors ruled him disabled and sent him to the ADA yard. What they didn't know: Rockhead had been informing on other gang members for some time. The rumors were starting to spread, and he knew it was only a matter of time before someone stuck a knife in his neck.

Joe had bumped into Rockhead and, instead of apologizing, said, "Hey, watch where you're walking."

Rockhead didn't hesitate. At well over six feet tall and two hundred-plus pounds, he grabbed Joe around the throat with both hands, lifted him clean off the ground, and choked him until he went limp.

It wasn't about killing him. Rockhead wanted to send a message—he was still the same hair-trigger killer everyone should respect and fear. And if he happened to rough up a parasitic serial killer along the way, all the better.

Strangely, Joe didn't seem to understand that in prison, even on an ADA yard, respect was everything. And in prison, the only answer for disrespect was violence.

I looked at him now. "Do you need help?"

His eyes scanned the yard until he found Rockhead. "That crazy bald bastard with all the tattoos? He grabbed me the other day, choked me unconscious, and just dropped me like garbage."

I couldn't help but think of all his victims he'd strangled and discarded. What Rockhead did felt like a dark kind of justice.

"You mean Rockhead?" I said. "He's not crazy. Why would he do that to you? Did you say something?"

Joe looked nervous. "No . . . well, yes, but not on purpose. I bumped into him, that's all." He wrung his hands. "And this morning, as soon as I put my things down, he walked up to my stuff and stole my coffee. Just took it."

I kept my voice calm. "Did you tell him to give it back? If you don't, he'll keep pushing. Next time, it won't be coffee. Next time, he'll rape you."

This sent him over the edge. "*Rape*? Why would he rape me? I'm an old man! Is he a homosexual?"

"No, Joe. He's a predator. Rape isn't about sex—it's about power. It's how he'll take your manhood, your dignity. He's testing you. If you let him take one thing, he'll come for more."

"That's nuts . . . all for bumping into him?"

"You can't let it go. You have to put a stop to it."

"I can't. He's too big. Can't I just pay him off?"

"You can, but that tells him you're weak. This isn't the regular world. The rules are different."

I stood to go.

"Wait," he said. "You can help me. We're friends. That's what friends do, right?"

I paused and then slowly sat back down. "What do you have in mind?"

"Tell him to leave me alone. Tell him you'll protect me."

"Joe, if I say that, I'm telling him I'll stop him. That's a threat."

"Please," he said, his voice cracking. "I don't want to be raped."

This was an opportunity I hadn't expected. But I had to play it carefully. If Rockhead suspected I had an agenda, that I was writing a book, he'd find a way to exploit it. He might try to blackmail me or expose my motives. Still, this was the perfect moment to demonstrate my power—to show Joe what I could do.

"I get it," I said. "You're asking me to stop him. Because you can't."

Joe nodded furiously.

I grew quiet, as if thinking about the situation. "If I do this, you need to keep your mouth shut. I mean really shut—like you've kept your mouth shut over the past fifty years about all those girls you killed."

He opened his mouth to protest, but I raised my hand. "Don't. I'm a criminal and a killer too. I see through that pathetic mask you've used to fool the cops and everyone else. If you lie to me, I'll step aside and let Rockhead rape you."

The threat finally sank in. Joe's hands trembled, his face drained of color.

"All right," I said. "I'll stop Rockhead. He won't touch you. But not a word. No matter what he says, you don't say shit. I'll be watching."

"Yes," he whispered. "I won't say anything."

But I knew better. Joe couldn't keep quiet—just what I was counting on.

I stood to leave. "I'll see you later, Joe."

"Wait! Let's talk about art." He clutched my portfolio to his chest like a lifeline.

"Bring it out tomorrow. And remember what I said."

As I walked away, I left him with something he had never carried before: the terrible burden of being a victim, the same burden his own victims never lived long enough to escape.

My journal: figuring out how to play the Rockhead situation.

7

The Setup

When yard was finally called, I went straight out, ready to put my plan in motion.

I placed my towel and tumbler of water on the ground, staking my claim. Then, breaking my routine, I hung my gym bag on the fence, the same as everyone else. I needed it to look casual, unremarkable. Like I'd done it a hundred times.

While waiting for the men to arrive, I ran through a light set of push-ups and burpees—just enough to work up a good sweat and leave a damp imprint on the cement.

As the gate opened and the men started filtering in, I slid into character, bringing to life the persona I'd perfected over more than three decades behind bars: cold-eyed, controlled, and quietly dangerous.

Joe was third in line, slumped in his wheelchair, visibly relieved. No sign of Rockhead—yet. But as soon as Joe reached the small corridor between the two yards, Rockhead rounded the corner and joined the line.

I moved fast. "How you doing, Joe?" I grabbed his chair by the armrests and lifted him through the gate. "I'm going to push you over by my gear right next to the fence. Stay in this chair and don't move, no matter what. Understand?"

He looked around frantically. "Is that guy coming out here? Is he gonna try something?"

"As I told you, he won't touch you. But you have to do exactly what

I say. Otherwise, you're on your own. He can rape you and I won't lift a finger. Got it?"

He nodded, mumbling to himself.

I rolled him over to my workout spot. When I grabbed Joe's bag from the back of his chair, I noticed my portfolio tucked inside. Perfect. I hung his bag next to mine, shielding my movements, and then reached into my bag and pulled out a lunch bag labeled "Bill 4-77." I slipped it into Joe's bag. Mission accomplished.

Now all I had to do was let the scene play out. I'd bet everything on both Joe and Rockhead acting true to form.

Sure enough, Rockhead entered the yard wearing his neon-green "Hearing Impaired" vest. He spotted Naso, who went stiff, a look of horror on his face. Smirking, Rockhead charged toward his wheelchair and shook it violently. Joe sprang to his feet, with more agility than I'd ever seen from him.

"Stop that!" he shouted. "What's wrong with you? Leave me alone!"

Grinning, Rockhead blew him a kiss and strolled over to the fence where the bags hung.

From a short distance away, I watched everything unfold. Rockhead, puffed up from terrifying Joe, didn't think twice. He reached into Joe's bag, pulled out the lunch bag of coffee and chocolates I'd planted, and stuffed it into his own bag. Then he reached in again and took my portfolio.

Hook baited, set, and swallowed.

Joe, now back in his wheelchair, locked eyes with Rockhead. Big mistake. Not one to let a challenge go unanswered, Rockhead stomped over to him and kicked the tumbler. It shot into the air and slammed against the concrete, shattering.

Another win.

I walked over, picked up the pieces, and stared at Rockhead. His brain was slowly catching up as I marched over to him.

He'd just broken a nonnegotiable prison rule: Disrespect a man's property and you disrespect the man.

His eyes dropped to the lid in my hand. The small green circle on top was my mark, and everyone knew it. Then his gaze shifted to the towel beneath his feet.

I moved in close, my eyes boring into his. "Hey, dickhead, what's your problem?"

He took a step back, and I followed.

"I said, what's your problem, motherfucker?"

He stepped back once again. "Brother, my bad. I'll pay for the tumbler—I didn't realize it was yours. Honest mistake. I'll make it up to you." He nodded toward Joe. "I thought it belonged to that piece of shit."

Right on cue, Joe jumped in. "He's a bully and a thief, Bill! He took your stuff from my bag."

I turned slowly to look at Joe. "What did you say?"

Joe stood, pointing. "Check his bag. He stole your things!"

I grabbed Rockhead's bag and yanked it from the fence.

"Hey, man, that's my fuckin' bag!" he yelled, coming my way.

I turned hard. "You gonna stop me?"

He stopped in his tracks.

"That's what I thought," I said.

I dumped the contents of his bag on the ground and held up my portfolio. "This yours?"

Rockhead shook his head.

I pointed to my name on the cover. "Can you read?"

Rockhead fidgeted, looking worried.

I held up the lunch bag. "What's this say? Either you're stupid or you meant to steal it—which is it?"

Joe couldn't help himself. "He's a thief. Yesterday he stole from me too!"

Rockhead lunged toward Joe, but I stepped between them. "Where the fuck you going? Your business is right here."

Cornered, Rockhead snapped. "This whole mess is because that snitch-rat motherfucker won't shut his mouth. But I'll fix that."

I leaned in so only he could hear me. "Snitching? Like you did with Terry, Rider, and your crew? Yeah, I know. You've been busy."

That hit home. He turned pale.

I gave him a frosty grin. "This is my yard now. You're in my house—and you owe me rent."

Rockhead clenched his jaw, calculating. He had two choices: take a swing and end up in the hospital or swallow his pride.

"You gonna call me out to my brothers?" he asked.

I smiled. "Keep your hands out of my shit and your business stays yours."

"I'll buy you a new tumbler. I'm sorry."

"Nice try. That just covers the cup. What about the rest of the stuff you stole?"

He shot a quick look at yard six, general population. They were watching. "What do you want, Bill? I didn't know it was yours. I fucked up—just name your price."

He tried to play it cool, but I could see the flicker of fear behind his eyes.

I shrugged. "Don't trip. If I think of something, you'll be the first to know."

I held my ground. Rockhead backed off, the swagger gone, his eyes fixed on the cement.

No punches or bloodshed.

And my stock had just skyrocketed in Joe's eyes. The truth I was after was one step closer.

Within minutes, Naso returned to being an obnoxious little prick, strutting around the yard. In his mind, having me as his "best friend" gave him license to do whatever the hell he wanted.

That was dangerous.

Rockhead might have let it go for now, but he wasn't a man known for restraint. If Joe pushed the wrong button, Rockhead would make his move and deal with me later. I couldn't let that happen. Joe needed a tight, short leash or he would get himself killed—and me too.

As the yard settled back into its rhythm, I found a quiet spot near the fence bordering yard six. The wall, topped with razor wire, was at my back. From where I sat, I had a clear view of everything and everyone.

Joe spotted me alone and, true to form, walked straight over to my bag, pulled out my portfolio, and headed my way as if nothing had happened.

"Thought this was a good time for us to talk," he said.

"Joe," I said, "did I tell you it was okay for you to go into my bag and take my things?"

He blinked.

"Listen closely. I just got through ripping someone apart for doing exactly that. Knock it off, or next time, I'll let Rockhead do whatever he wants to you."

His eyes grew wide.

"And while we're at it," I said, "stop prancing around like a fuckin' peacock. You're not in San Francisco in the seventies. This isn't your playground. Every man on this yard is a killer. You piss one off and they won't hesitate to slit your throat. Have you forgotten already how close you came to being raped—or worse?"

His mouth opened, then closed. He looked down, chastened.

"So why'd you come over here with my portfolio?"

"I don't know," he mumbled. "You sound mad. I don't want you to be mad at me."

For a second, I almost felt sorry for the old man. The fear in his voice sounded real. He seemed weak and pathetic.

Almost.

I reminded myself who I was talking to. Joseph Naso. This man wasn't harmless. This man was Joseph Naso—a monster who had fooled everyone who ever underestimated him. That's how he got them. That's how he killed.

"I'm not mad, Joe. I said I'd help you, and I never break my word. That's the difference between me and all these other guys." I motioned toward the yard. "But you've got to stop acting like no one can touch you. Look at what happened with Rockhead. You didn't handle it right. That can get you killed."

He stood there like a scolded child, his eyes fixed on his feet.

I gave his arm a light punch. "Forget all these assholes for now. Let's talk about art."

His face lit up, and he opened up my portfolio with care, revealing Post-it notes on several pages. "Let's sit over there," he said, pointing to the bench in the far corner of the yard, as far away as possible from everyone, where he felt safest.

We started with art, but it didn't take long before Joe's ego pulled him into darker territory. He brought up Foxy Roxy again, one of his "girls," but this time, he didn't linger lovingly on her red hair and beautiful body. His voice hardened, the easy charm gone.

"She was my birthday present," he said, his grin tight. "Two days after I turned forty-three. Said she was going to nursing school. Lying whore."

He leaned back, savoring the memory. "I gave her what she deserved."

It wasn't the full story, not even close. But something had shifted. The Rockhead setup had worked. Joe now believed I could protect him and, more importantly, that I *wanted* to.

That conversation marked the moment Joe's mask began to slip—for good. Three months later, he finally told me why the women had to die.

And once I knew, there was no going back.

8

The Rain

The forecast had called for wind and rain, and the sky delivered. Thunder rumbled as the loudspeaker announced yard release. It was miserably dark and wet, and I doubted anyone would be stupid enough to go out in it, except me.

But I wasn't the only one. As unlikely as it seemed, two others from the ADA yard braved the storm: David Carpenter and Gary Hines in his wheelchair.

After checking they didn't need anything, I stretched and started my run. The downpour hammered me, soaking me to the skin. In just shorts and running shoes, I pushed through the sheets of water. When I glanced up, the gunner in his tower caught my eye and waved, probably thinking I was insane.

Half an hour later, as I came around the final lap, the door to East Block opened. Joe rolled out in his wheelchair, his jaw clenched, clearly pissed at the wind-driven rain.

I let out a hollow laugh. How the fuck did I end up in a place like this?

"Morning, Joe." I took hold of his chair. "Where'd you like to go?"

He waved a hand vaguely, but I knew the drill: bag on the fence, him beside it. Today, I'd keep him under the awning to stay out of the rain.

As I unhooked his bag from the chair, he stood up. "Let me ask you something."

His appearance had been declining for weeks. The little bit of hair he had left wasn't combed, his clothes were rumpled and stained, and he smelled sour.

"What's on your mind, Joe?"

"You know that chick Andrews, the sports reporter?"

Erin Andrews. The news had been everywhere—her lawsuit against a hotel for allowing a stalker to secretly film her nude through a peephole in her room.

"Yes, I—"

"The broad sues a hotel for millions," he said, his words edged with contempt. "What a fuckin' whore. If she stayed home and took care of her husband and kids like a good wife, none of this would've happened. She deserved it." He barked out a harsh laugh.

I scanned the yard. The wind was pushing rain under the awning, drenching Joe. "Let's go under the gun rail where it's dry."

Once we were clear of the downpour, I locked his wheelchair in place. "So this woman is at fault because a pervert filmed her in her hotel room? That make sense to you?"

He shrugged. "She was naked."

I fixed my eyes on him. "Everyone gets naked in their own room—to take a shower, change clothes, use the bathroom, whatever. Hell, she could dance naked all night if she wants. What right does anyone have to film her secretly and put it online for the world to see? How could that be her fault?"

He shook his head. "No, no, no—you don't get it."

Naso wasn't interested in arguing. He simply wanted to get it off his chest, and I needed to listen. "Okay, Joe. Tell me again."

"I see her on TV, and I know by looking at her that she's a whore. I can always tell. That's my skill. I know who needs to be cleaned."

"'Cleaned'?" The word stopped me cold.

"Fuckin' whore deserved to be seen for what she really is. Hold on. I'll show you."

He hurried over to his bag on the fence and pulled out a folder. When he turned around, I caught the unmistakable bulge in his pants.

Back beside me, he slid an eight-by-ten photo from the folder and handed it to me.

"What's this?" I asked.

"What do you see?"

The woman in the photo was in her twenties, her makeup and long hair from the late sixties or early seventies. She was lying on orange shag carpet, partially nude, her eyes closed.

Something about it felt off. I stared at the creepy scene, trying to figure out what Joe was fishing for.

He handed me another image. "What about this one?" He smiled, all yellow teeth and sagging skin. But his eyes turned sharp and piercing, the way they always did when he crossed back into the darkness he never truly left.

The second photo showed the same woman in the same setting, maybe minutes later. But something had changed. Something was missing.

Then I remembered what he'd said when I first saw his work: *Like a surgeon. I leave only what's necessary.*

"So you removed what was in the way?"

"Yes." He exhaled heavily as if relieved of a great burden only he had carried. "You understand my work."

When he handed me the next set of photos, the truth became clear.

A new woman, another victim. In the first photo, she clutched a phone receiver and looked back at the camera with a flirty tilt of her chin. Blond and pretty in an unremarkable way. Taken sometime in the seventies. The kind of photo you'd expect in an amateur's portfolio.

The second photo showed her in red lingerie, lying on a bed, eyes closed.

This time, I was sure: Her eyes weren't simply closed—she was dead.

Joe studied me closely. "The only way to get a perfect shot is to remove the part that lies," he said. "She's no longer a money-loving whore. She's pure now. Innocent."

I switched back to the girl holding the phone.

He sneered. "I watched her for weeks. Four, five, sometimes six men a night. She was selling herself." He coughed roughly. "She smiled like she liked it, but she was lying. Fuckin' whore needed to be cleaned. Now she's honest. Now she's art."

"But, Joe, isn't it possible to get the perfect shot without removing who she is?"

"Absolutely not. Real art can't be staged or compromised."

I stared at the photo and then back at him, this frail old man with murder in his eyes.

On that rainy morning, something inside Naso cracked open.

He started talking—in vivid detail, sometimes in fragments, sometimes out of order, like old film reels spliced together the wrong way. One victim might surface in a half-sentence, only to reappear months later in a full confession.

But I kept him going.

Every story was a thread. And slowly, at my own risk, I began tying them together.

The portraits of his victims emerged slowly, one by one.

And what they revealed will haunt me forever.

PART TWO
THE VICTIMS

1) GIRL NEAR HELDSBURG MENDOCINO CO.

2) Girl NEAR PORT COSTA

3) Girl NEAR LOGANITAS

4) Girl ON MT TAM

5) Girl FROM MIAMI NEAR DOWN PENINSULA

6) Girl FROM Berkeley

7) LADY FROM 859 LEAVENWORTH

8) Girl IN ~~Danville~~ WOODLAND (NEAR NEVADA COUNTY)

9) Girl FROM LINDA (YUBA County)

10) Girl FROM MRSV. (Cemetery)

Joseph Naso's handwritten List of Ten murder victims.

9

Roxene: The Hunt

The first real thread he gave me was about Roxy.

By then, I already knew the short version: his "birthday present," a redhead with the body of a model. Weeks earlier, he'd dangled that much in front of me like bait.

Now we sat apart from the others, the cool air between us sharpening his focus. He leaned forward, lowering his voice, guarding the truth he'd kept buried for decades.

He didn't start with her name. He started with the city and the street.

And in his mind, he was back there. Behind the wheel, scanning faces, easing off the gas to spot her.

All that mattered was the hunt.

And he wanted me to see it through his eyes.

DATE: Friday, December 17, 1976
LOCATION: Oakland, California
NASO'S LIST: #3. The Girl near Loganitas [Lagunitas]
VICTIM: Roxene "Foxy Roxy" Roggasch
Part One: The Hunt

International Boulevard buzzed with the usual filth—drug deals on the corners, addicts slumped in the doorways, girls pacing for their next hit or their next john. The cool night air was heavy with urine and sweat.

Joe cruised slowly, scanning the sidewalks. Women approached his car, but he waved them off.

He wasn't there for them. He was there for the redhead.

He'd seen her the day before. A quick smile, the long line of her neck—then she was gone, and she hadn't left his mind since. He could already picture her in his studio, her young body responding under his hands. Her image would be sealed forever in his lens.

Joe carried memberships in the Professional Photographers of America, the California association, and the Greater Bay Area group, but the one-bedroom on MacArthur Boulevard wasn't for that. No headshots. No family sittings. It was where he took the women he bought, raped, and—if they inspired him—immortalized in his "perfect portraits."

Joe's car crawled along the curb.

Where are you?

Maybe he'd misread her. Maybe she wasn't for sale.

As if on cue, a large blue Buick pulled over up ahead. The redhead got out and leaned into the passenger window, chatting with the driver and laughing. Joe's pulse quickened. She *was* working.

The traffic forced him past, and he circled the block, panicking. Someone else might claim her first.

When he got back, she'd disappeared. As soon as he parked, another girl slid away from the wall and leaned into Joe's passenger door window, her breasts pressed high.

"How's it going, honey? You lookin' for a date?"

"I'm trying to find someone."

"I'm someone." She winked. "You like my tits?"

"They're lovely, dear, but I'm after a particular redhead who got dropped off here a few minutes ago."

Just then, she emerged from a nearby store.

"That's her!" Joe said, nearly shouting.

The girl called out, "Hey, Roxy, this guy's looking for you."

Roxy's face lit up at the sound of her name. She glided over to his car and crouched down by his window, her perfume cutting through the exhaust and street rot. "Hey, Daddy, you lookin' for me?"

Joe took her in like a work of art—her mouth, skin tone, body type—but most of all, the deceit in her eyes. Yes, she was the one.

"I sure am, gorgeous." His tone sharpened. "How old are you?"

He held his breath. Seventeen meant she was untouchable. In his world, child molesters were the lowest of the low—sick scumbags. Children were off-limits. Always.

"Don't worry, honey, I'm eighteen." She smiled, tilting her head. "So what's it gonna be—lips or hips?"

"Get in."

Once inside, she pressed herself against him, rubbing him through his pants. "Whatcha got, hon? This for me?"

He pulled away from the curb and headed for a deserted factory lot he'd used before. Her perfume and the promise in her touch made it impossible to think of anything else—exactly how he liked it. The higher the anticipation, the better the release. She was everything he'd imagined.

But one more thing had to fall into place before she became more than just another hooker he'd paid for sex. The key was deception. Looks and attitude were easy to size up. The lies took longer. They had to be brought into focus, the image sharpened until the truth emerged.

After sex, Joe eased into the questions—each one a calculated move toward the answer he wanted.

"Hey, baby, how long you been doing this? I mean . . . you're beautiful. You could have any guy you want. You could be a model."

"I just started. I need the money for tuition. I'm going to nursing school."

She said it lightly, unaware of the change in him. In the darkness of the car, he fixed on her like prey, his body wound tight, his voice flat and controlled. "Can't your family help you out? You're so young."

"My parents are dead. I don't know who my family is. I was adopted."

Her response was too quick, the words sliding out like something rehearsed. A lie.

"I'm sorry to hear that. Maybe I can help you. What's your name?"

She scoffed. "What do you mean, 'help me'? Are you gonna be my sugar daddy? My name's Roxy."

Joe ignored the jab. "I'm a professional photographer and successful artist. I'd like to pay you for a session or two. You have features I'd love to capture on film."

He pulled out his wallet, peeled off a ten and a twenty, and handed them to the girl, along with his business card. "See? One hundred percent legit."

She studied the card. "A model, huh? Wouldn't that be something."

For a moment, she let herself imagine what that would be like—the very thing Joe counted on.

That fantasy would cost her.

Over the next week, Joe parked just off International Boulevard and watched her through the long lens of his camera. Seven men a night, sometimes more, each one getting the same easy charm she'd used on him.

"Fuckin' whore," he muttered. "Your turn's coming soon."

But the holidays got in the way. Joe was also a husband and father, and Judith knew nothing of his other life. With David and Charles home on Christmas vacation from school, he wore the mask of a family man.

Still, a few times, he slipped back to International Boulevard, not for sex, but to watch her through his lens. He could wait. Patience always paid off.

By early January, the boys were back in school. On the seventh, Joe's forty-third birthday, he ate dinner with his family at an Italian place in San Francisco. Outwardly, he was a normal middle-aged man celebrating with his wife and kids.

Inside, Roxy was still with him—the men she'd taken, the smile, the laugh, the lies behind the way she drew them close. Heat rose in him, anger tangled with desire, feeding the truth he'd carried since he was a teenager: women were whores, to be used, abused, and thrown away.

The next day, Joe drove to his small apartment in Oakland to prepare. This wasn't about calming nerves—he'd done this before. It was about making sure every detail on his "To-Do" list was exactly right.

For hours, he staged his little studio of horrors. Sheets over the windows. Lights set. Cameras loaded. Mannequins posed. One wore a red wig.

"Please come in," he said to it. "Can I get you a drink?"

In his mind, it said, "I'm nervous. I've never modeled before."

"That's very natural, my dear. Let me put on some music."

Joe bowed to the mannequin, picked it up, and danced to a waltz only he could hear. In his fantasy, they were at the Regency Hotel in San Francisco and everyone stopped to admire them. The men envied him. The women wanted to be her.

He was the famous photographer who transformed ordinary whores into perfect portraits.

The music ended. Joe carried the mannequin to the couch. "Let's sit a while. I'd like to know a little more about you."

Over the next hour, Joe dressed it in lingerie and took photographs in different positions, his erection growing with each shot.

"Make me yours, Joe," he heard it say.

He kissed it deeply and thrust his hips against it until he shuddered in release.

Then a thin, boyish giggle slipped out before he clamped his hands around its throat, shaking it. "Fuckin' whore. Fuckin' bitch."

When he finally stopped, he looked down at the mannequin, grinning. "Foxy Roxy."

10

Roxene: The Trap

DATE: Sunday, January 9, 1977
LOCATION: Oakland, California
NASO'S LIST: #3. The Girl near Loganitas [Lagunitas]
VICTIM: Roxene "Foxy Roxy" Roggasch
Part Two: The Trap

Two days after his birthday, Joe was ready for the real celebration. That night, he would be with the woman he wanted most and make her his forever.

International Boulevard glowed—storefronts, clubs, bars, cars prowling for business—but the street was quiet, just as he'd planned. Fewer witnesses meant fewer risks. He drove straight to the liquor store where he'd seen her before. She was there, leaning against a phone booth.

He pulled to the curb and rolled down the passenger window. The cold January air carried her perfume—White Shoulders. He'd bought a bottle of it after their first night. One whiff and she was with him again.

"You come for some company?" she asked, her voice soft with fatigue.

"I sure did."

Roxy scooted in beside him. "Where're you taking me, honey?"

"To my place, a couple of blocks over. We'll have some fun, take a few pictures like I said before. I'll throw in another fifty."

She touched his thigh. "That sounds nice. You'll have to show me what to do."

"Sure thing. I'll walk you through it. You'll be perfect. Unforgettable."

At his apartment door, she paused, a flicker of doubt in her eyes. He gave her a mild, reassuring smile and flipped on the lights. She seemed to relax as she stepped inside, taking in what looked like an artist's studio—cluttered just enough to feel authentic.

"Why the sheets on the windows, Daddy?"

"For lighting." He pointed to the lamps aimed at the couch covered in a red sheet.

She noticed the mannequins and touched the one with the red wig, laughing nervously. Joe grabbed a camera and snapped a shot. The sound made her relax. She even posed.

"Hold that," Joe said, taking a few more.

He handed her some lingerie. "Bathroom's down the hall."

When she returned, she followed every direction—sitting and lying on the couch, draping pantyhose over her shoulders and around her neck.

"Now, look past me, to the left," he said. Click. "Good." Click.

Setting the camera down, he kissed her neck and stroked her legs. "You're beautiful," he said.

Soon the lingerie was on the floor and he was on top of her. She worked him with practiced ease, not noticing when he reached for a heavy camera lens.

The first blow stunned her, but she fought back—far tougher than her small frame suggested. Two more strikes and she crumpled. Breathing hard, Joe finished on her, then rammed pantyhose into her mouth, gagged her tight with another pair, and bound her wrists.

He rifled through the girl's purse, pocketing the seventy-eight dollars and her identification and tossing the rest aside.

Picking up his Nikon, he waited for her to stir. When her eyelids fluttered open, the fear was pure—raw, unposed. She thrashed on the couch, moaning, her head snapping side to side in a frantic bid to break free. Tears streaked her face.

The sound of her muffled cries and the violent twitch of her body only sharpened his focus. It was everything he wanted: the mask gone, the truth laid bare. He moved in close, circling her, snapping frame after frame, drinking in her terror.

Pleased with the shots, he lowered the camera and looked into the mirror. In his mind, the balding middle-aged man with glasses and a paunch had vanished. Staring back at him was a young, vibrant artist in his prime.

"I've got something for you, Roxene Roggasch," he told her. "You'll love it. Fuckin' whore."

Joe hauled her to the floor by the hair, gripping it like a set of handles, and entered her again. "Yeah, fuckin' bitch, you love it, don't you."

He let go and slammed his fist into the side of her head—a sharp blow to stop her fight. Her eyes rolled back. Wanting to heighten his pleasure, he moved off her to turn her over. In that instant, she snapped her leg up and kicked him hard in the groin. She staggered to her feet, but he closed the distance in a single step and yanked her down.

"Not so fast, Roxy. We're not done yet."

He looped the pantyhose around her neck and pulled tight as he thrust into her one last time. When she spasmed and went limp, the giggles burst out of him—high and giddy—as he reached for another camera.

He posed her corpse on the couch, adjusted the lights, and worked the angles until he had the perfect portrait. No lies now.

Joe made a cup of coffee and drank it beside her. "I have a nice place to put you," he said, resting an arm across her shoulders.

He got dressed and bagged her belongings, keeping a pair of panties for himself. Then he tied her legs with a belt and carried her to his car in the alley. A slow scan of the shadows assured him no one was watching before he slid her into the trunk.

He slipped out of the dark alley and onto Highway 580 toward Richmond. No hurry. He hummed along with the radio.

At the far end of the Richmond–San Rafael Bridge, the brightly lit towers of San Quentin rose into the night sky. Joe looked away. Prisons were for stupid, careless men.

He turned onto Lagunitas Road, parked his car in a dark stretch, and sat listening to the engine tick as it cooled. Certain he was alone, he dragged the redhead from the trunk and into some thick bushes. She hit the ground with a dull thud.

"Have a nice life, fuckin' bitch."

He shut the trunk softly, the night swallowing the sound.

> he also picked her up. Said had been
> with her before. picked up on International
> Blvd, (speaks in obsessive manner about
> making her perfect)
> Took her to small studio for a
> modeling session. He agreed to pay for
> her time and pay her as a model.
> Says she seemed excited about being a
> model, but knew she was only interested
> in money. Called her Foxy Roxy many
> times, and "whore". also openly rubbed,
> touched and masturbated which he told me
> how he killed her.

My journal: Roxene "Foxy Roxy" Roggasch.

11

The List

The Roxene confession opened a new door. I began asking Joe questions I never would have dared before, and he answered without hesitation. But I had to tread carefully. I didn't know yet how far I could go with our newfound friendship.

Still, I came prepared to test the limits. One morning, we sat at our usual table away from the others, and I brought up his list of ten murders, the one the police found at his house.

"Joe, why was Roxene Roggasch number three? Was she the third woman you murdered?"

He burst out laughing.

"What's so funny?"

Joe shook his head. "No. That list isn't based on dates or any order the cops would figure out." He studied me, as if waiting to see if I'd catch on.

"Okay," I said. "So what *is* it based on?"

As he often did, he didn't respond directly to my question. "It's funny. The cops made such a big deal about that damn list."

"You have to admit—it did seal the case for them."

"Pure dumb luck. That list of ten wasn't a record of my murders. The real list—the one I kept for years—got stolen when some asshole broke into my storage unit." He waved it off. "What they found was just a game I played, remembering some of the girls I'd been with."

He leaned closer. "How many girls you been with? Thirty? Forty? Well, I've been with hundreds. Hundreds of whores. All of them different. Sure, some reminded me of others, but out of your thirty or forty, I bet you could give me a top five. The ones who stood out."

His eyes glinted as he grinned. "That fuckin' list wasn't about murder. It was my top ten fucks!" He chuckled, shaking his head. "It was just me, drunk one night, writing down favorites. Never crossed my mind anyone would find it—let alone connect it."

"But you did kill all of them?"

"Sure did," he said flatly. "And sixteen more."

A jolt shot through me.

Twenty-six.

More than twice what investigators had on record. Six solved. Twenty unsolved. Twenty women whose names and faces were still buried in cold files. And now I might be holding the key to unlocking them.

I gave nothing away. "That list was your top ten, and they span a timeline of about what? Fifteen years?"

He stood from the table. "Let's walk. It's a nice day."

We paced near the basketball court, the yard alive with the usual activities—dominoes, card games, idle talk. I used the noise as cover, pushing for more, losing track of time.

"Joe, did you call—"

He cut me off with a sideways glance, his voice low and even. "You ask a lot of questions."

Exactly the boundary I'd dreaded. I pivoted fast, feeding his vanity. "Well, it's exciting to hear about your work, Joe. You're a true artist."

That did the trick—he beamed, pride softening his expression.

We walked on in silence, each step reminding me how thin the line was. Probe too hard, and he'd retreat. Hold back, and I might never get this close to the truth again.

"I'm curious about something," I said carefully. "The reports said an anonymous caller tipped the cops about Roxene's body the night it happened. Was that you? They seemed to think so."

His laugh was flat. "No. You kidding? Never happened. That's them jamming puzzle pieces where they don't fit."

Someone had reported a man dumping what looked like a body near Fairfax, along Sir Frances Drake Boulevard. A deputy sheriff responded and found Roxy in the thick brush—naked, her feet tied with a belt, pantyhose still wrapped around her neck.

Joe's jaw tightened. "She was a nasty little whore I enjoyed fucking and making perfect. But I didn't make that call. Someone must've seen me, though I swear I was alone. No cars passed." He paused. "With today's cameras everywhere? I'd never get away with it now."

"You know, a lot of artists go to galleries to watch the reaction to their work. Some say killers insert themselves into investigations—call in tips, show up at the scene—just to feel in control."

"That's true and false," he said. "I never cared about being part of an investigation. Out of sight, out of mind. That's how I kept it. But sometimes, weeks or even years later, I'd drive back at night. If she was a favorite, I'd park nearby, lie down where I left her, and masturbate."

He stopped abruptly and faced me, his eyes sharp. "Tell me about one of yours. If we're sharing, I wanna hear one of yours."

I hadn't seen that coming.

My pulse spiked, but I kept my expression steady. Refusing wasn't an option—it could shatter the trust I'd built.

"Of course, as you know," I said slowly, buying a few seconds, "I'm here because I murdered a woman."

"Yeah, and that's good!" He pumped his fist. "Really good. Women are vile—they need to be put in their place. But I want a kill no one else knows about."

I nodded as if agreeing. I had to come up with something fast, something Joe couldn't see through.

"Fair enough," I said. "For me, it's about being an apex predator. To kill is to dominate another predator just as dangerous as I am."

I brought up Rockhead as an example. "Remember what happened? I didn't need violence to dominate him, but he knew it was there, implied. On the streets, violence is never implied—it's lived."

> Spoke of list of 10. said Cops
> got it all wrong. List they found is
> not murder list. Its a game he played
> with himself to list his Top 10. Said
> his Kill number is 26, He Killed 26
> women in Bay area, Los Angeles. Las Vegas
> and New york. ~ Raped in phil. Ny

My journal: Naso's List of Ten murders. Total kills: twenty-six.

Joe leaned in, hungry for more.

I'd read about killers who paired off in prison, feeding each other's sickness—men like Lawrence Bittaker and Roy Norris. They'd met at the California Men's Colony in San Luis Obispo, considered by many to be a country club for "soft" time. After they were released, their shared fantasies of abducting, raping, and torturing teenage girls became a reality, and five victims paid the price.

It was the same principle I now dangled in front of Joe: a partnership. But would he buy it?

I drew a deep breath and began, pulling together a story on the fly—part truth, part invention, laced with just enough grit to pass for real.

"I was only seventeen at the time," I told Joe. "Already one of Southern California's top high-end car thieves. One afternoon, two gang members came into my warehouse, demanding payment for protection. I told them to come back that night for the money. What they didn't know was that I'd planned to make sure neither of them walked away."

I painted the picture—how I trapped them under the half-lifted garage door, knocked one out with a torque wrench and cracked the other's skull so hard it sounded like a watermelon splitting. How I dragged them inside, cuffed the first guy to my toolbox, and drove a sharpened railroad spike into the chest of the second.

When the cuffed guy came to and saw his partner, the panic was instant—a piercing scream that rattled through the empty warehouse.

"He begged," I said. "And cried. Pissed himself. I made him understand what fear really is."

Joe nodded vigorously, clapping his hands.

"Then I wrapped a half-inch rope around his neck and pulled. His face—"

"You can feel the body spasm through the rope, right? The death shakes. But it's much better if you're inside them!"

A part of me wanted to strangle him then and there, but I masked my disgust. None of this was easy. Pretending to be like Joe forced me into a place I never wanted to go—into his fantasies, his cruelty, his view of women as prey.

I hated every second—but I needed the truth he dangled in front of me.

Because what I wanted even more than another confession or count to add to his tally was the answer to the question that haunted every investigator and every victim's family: why.

Why did Joseph Naso kill? Why did he hate women so much that murder became his obsession?

To find that answer, I'd have to go deeper. I'd have to live inside his madness—and take the scars with me.

In the months that followed, he doled out more stories, one victim here, another there. Sometimes, he carried a battered folder, stuffed with photos and scraps, proof of his kills.

But the real beginning stayed buried—until he asked me for something most men would never dare.

12

The Origins

It started casually. One morning, Joe pulled me aside, lowering his voice like he was letting me in on a secret. "Is there anything you *can't* get?"

I shrugged. "Depends. I've got friends in high and low places. I can get magazines, small things. What do you want?"

His eyes darted around the yard before locking on mine. "Porn. The kind with women tied up. Screaming. In pain."

I didn't flinch. "Won't be cheap. And the guys who move that stuff want cash."

"Cash isn't a problem. I want what I want." He hesitated, then leaned closer. "A couple more things—and this has to stay between us, okay? A pair of women's pantyhose. Underwear too. Used, if possible. And red, with matching lipstick."

I let it hang there. "You're serious."

"Dead serious."

I nodded slowly. "Fine. But understand—I'm writing a book about you. I'll include everything. Even this." I held his gaze. "I'm thinking of calling it *The Portrait Killer.*"

To my surprise, he clapped his hands. "Yeah! I love it. When's it coming out? I'll sign a copy."

It didn't matter if he believed me. I'd told him the truth, and he said yes. The rest was on him.

The next day, I slipped a note to a convict housed near Lawrence

Bittaker. On death row, Bittaker was the go-to broker for anything obscene. By evening, I had my answer: $450 cash for two hardcore bondage magazines, two pairs of panties, pantyhose, and lipstick.

Two weeks later, the package arrived. When I smuggled it out to Joe, he caressed the panties, smiling like a man reunited with a lover. Then he vanished—for seven straight days. I didn't have to guess why.

When he finally reappeared, he was beaming. As soon as the gate was locked and the guards went back inside, Naso asked me to push him as far away from the others as possible. We stopped near the basketball court. Standing, his back to the yard, he looped his fingers into his waistband and pulled up.

He was wearing the panties.

I stared—not at the lace peeking above his pants, but at the faint smear of lipstick on his mouth.

He grinned, almost playful, like a child showing off stolen candy.

"How do you feel, Joe?"

"Like me," he said.

It was the closest thing I'd ever seen to joy on his face.

Behind the grin, I could see something pressing to the surface— something he'd been holding back.

He wanted to explain. And I let him.

"It started in Rochester, New York," he said. "I'd sneak into my mom's dresser, try on her underwear and heels. The first time I got hard, I didn't even know what it was."

His mother knew. She caught him one morning and exploded. The belt came down again and again as she spat the word "sick" at him. He was nine. After that, she mocked him as "Miss Josey," her "special daughter." The welts healed. The shame stayed. From then on, she wasn't just his mother—she was the enemy.

By then, he was already stealing from vendors on the streets for two years—gum, toys, candy—anything he could get his hands on. "It was exciting," he said. "Better than being in the house with her."

Naso, wanted to explain himself and I let him. He told me, about when he first wanting to try on his mothers underwear. and heels. He was a young boy, and couldn't explain why he found womens underwear so appealing, only that when he put them on. He was immediately aroused.

He explained his mother caught him wearing her things and beat him, as well as began calling him Her daughter, which sent him into a fit of rage.

(He suddenly told me he knew early on he would kill women. - I aske

My journal: Naso explained his underwear fetish.

His father was gone most of the time, working long hours to keep food on the table during the Depression. That left Joe under his mother's grip.

One morning, he struck back. She adored her yellow finch, listening to it sing every day. While she was outside hanging laundry, Joe opened the cage.

"I grabbed it," he told me, curling his hand as if the memory were still alive in his palm. "Crushed it just like that."

When his mother discovered the bird, she broke down sobbing. Joe laughed. He stood at the window and watched as she carried the tiny body into the yard and buried it.

"Watching her cry . . . I liked that." He smiled at the memory.

Soon he was shoplifting women's underwear and wearing it secretly in his room. When his mother caught him again, she ripped the items from his body and shredded them with her bare hands. Seeing his erection, she went into a frenzy, beating him with a kitchen ladle and calling him vile names until he crumpled on the floor.

"She hated me for it," he muttered, the words flat. "But I hated her more."

By twelve he'd already mastered the art of slipping through neighborhoods unnoticed—lifting lingerie off clotheslines, watching women through their windows at night. Shame and rage tangled with arousal until they were indistinguishable.

One afternoon, he came home early from caddying and heard sounds coming from his parents' bedroom. He crept around back and peered through the open window.

His mother was on her hands and knees, wearing nothing but stockings. Behind her, the neighborhood mechanic drove into her hard, sweat shining down his back.

Without thinking, Joe started touching himself, caught between lust and fury. Then he heard her voice, urgent and breathless: "Choke me."

The man's hands slid from her shoulders to her throat. She arched, gasping, while he squeezed. She climaxed with a groan.

Seventy years later, the rage was still raw. Joe clenched and un-clenched his hands, rubbing himself in front of me. "She was a fuckin' whore," he spat. "Walked around all proper, criticizing me, humiliat-ing me. Wouldn't let my dad touch her. But she let that creep pound into her. Fuckin' bitch."

His face twisted, his voice thick with venom.

The vision of his mother choking under another man's hands burned itself into him. For months afterward, Joe replayed it every night, jerking off to the memory until it dulled. Then he went looking for replacements.

He prowled the streets after dark, slipping into yards like a shadow. Clotheslines became his hunting ground. He stole panties, slips, and bras, wearing them as he crouched outside bedroom windows. Night after night, he spied on women while they sleep, sometimes catching them having sex.

"They were all liars," he told me, his lip curling. "Conniving bitches hiding behind masks of respectability. But I could see through it. I knew the truth."

In his mind, the underwear wasn't theft—it was conquest. The spy-ing wasn't trespass—it was exposure. He convinced himself he was the one man immune to the deception, the only one who could control women the way they "deserved."

Soon it wasn't enough to spy. At sixteen, he needed to touch and destroy. He lit fires—trash cans, then fields, then abandoned buildings. He escalated to pets, snaring strays and neighborhood cats, tormenting them until they stilled in his hands. Each act was a rehearsal.

On the surface, though, he passed for an ordinary teenager. He played sports, kept up decent grades, and cheered for the Yankees. He even had a girlfriend. He blended in perfectly, hiding in the open.

But the rituals had taken root, and there was no turning back. That spring in 1950, chance came calling—on a rare day his mother wasn't home.

Joe was about to step inside after school when an older girl with a laundry basket caught his eye and walked toward him. "You want clothes wash, home clean?" she asked in broken English. "I Sophia. I do clean."

He smiled at the dark Spanish girl with wide hips and eager eyes. "How much?"

She quoted a price, and he waved her through the door to get started.

When she reached his room, he leaned in and tried to kiss her. She turned her head away, laughing softly. "Not now, I'm working."

To Joe, that meant yes but later. He didn't want to wait. He shoved her onto the bed and pulled up her dress. She pushed against him, whispering "no" again and again. When he forced himself inside her, she froze. He took that as consent.

When he finished, she pulled her underwear up with shaking hands, tears sliding down her cheeks. He reached to kiss her again, but she clawed free, bolting half-dressed into the street and leaving her basket behind.

Joe shrugged, stretched out on his bed, and fell asleep.

That year marked the beginning of his terror on women.

13

The Rapes

Joseph Naso was no longer just a boy with a fetish. He was a rapist. The attack on Sophia had been a crime of opportunity. She stepped into his house with a laundry basket, and he took what he wanted, learning that women could be used like objects—nothing more than flesh to satisfy his needs. From then on, the line between desire and violence was gone.

For many rapists, the act itself satisfies their appetite. But for Joe, it was only the beginning. To escalate from rape to murder requires a reservoir of rage most people can't even imagine. Joe carried that rage inside him all the time—against his mother, against women in general, against himself.

Even then, patterns were already visible. He needed control, not just over women but over everything. Decades later, I'd see the same compulsion in his cell. He moved the junk from one corner to the next without pause or purpose. He hoarded everything that grabbed his attention—scraps of paper, empty milk cartons, clothes he never wore—until his cell was so cluttered and foul the guards skipped it during searches. If he couldn't complete these rituals, his frustration boiled over into violent outbursts.

Likewise, he was always changing the notes he took, his pictures, and even his patterns of walking. Yet, nothing was orderly or clean, not even himself. His personal hygiene was horrific.

And through it all, he carried himself as if he were a man of great importance, a prize for women, admired by men. That was Joe: disorder and delusion layered on top of a predator's mind.

But disorders don't explain twenty-six murders. Joe's crimes weren't accidents or breakdowns. They were deliberate—planned, stalked, and executed without regret.

After Sophia fled from his room, Joe quickly realized that rape was far more satisfying than spying on women, lighting fires, torturing animals, or stealing underwear. He never stopped stealing underwear—he would keep doing that until his arrest six decades later—but now he'd found the act that fed both his fantasies and his rage.

Almost immediately, he began hunting. On the outside, he was still a regular teenager with a girlfriend, decent grades, and sports to play. Normal was his camouflage. But behind that cover, he was looking for victims.

Joe didn't stalk alleys or break into houses, nor did he wear a mask and ambush strangers. He picked up hitchhikers or dated women, charming them into trusting him. They saw his face. He acted like a gentleman. Then, when the moment came, he turned—grabbing and raping, sometimes choking them until they passed out.

For Joe, it was never about lust. It was about control. In his delusion, he convinced himself women wanted him too. They said no, they cried, they fought—but in Joe's mind, he was giving them what they "really" wanted.

Once, after a brutal assault, he even drove the girl home and met her mother at the door, smiling like the perfect suitor. He believed the illusion himself: Joe the ladies' man, not Joe the predator.

By the early 1950s, he had already raped several women. With a car, he expanded his hunting ground beyond Rochester. Buffalo was a favorite spot, where hitchhiking girls lined the roads.

One day in August 1951, at only seventeen, he spotted a girl thumbing a ride along the 490. She was Black—a boundary most rapists at the time didn't cross—but Joe didn't hesitate.

He pulled over.

"You going into Buffalo?" she asked.

"I sure am," he said, smiling.

When she slid into the seat, he said, "My name is Joe."

"I'm Mary—after the Virgin Mary. I'm Catholic."

The words pricked at Joe, though he didn't understand why.

He drove them to a wooded area and parked. At first, it was harmless talk. He flattered her. She laughed, unbothered by his presence. He was just another teenager flirting with her.

But when he kissed her and tried to lift up her skirt, she grabbed his hand. "No, that's not happening."

Joe tried again, harder this time, and she pushed him off.

"I said no."

His hand shot to her throat. He punched her across the face, then shoved her down and raped her. She cried, begged him to stop. For Joe, the begging only fed his arousal. Control was the high.

Once he finished, he switched back to the charming teenager, speaking softly, like they were on a date. "We should see a movie tomorrow. I'll pick you up after school."

Mary didn't say a word. As soon as he stopped, she flew out of the car and ran.

Joe pulled away from the scene, muttering, "Fuckin' whore's no Virgin Mary." From beneath the seat, he retrieved the panties he'd stuffed there, pressed them to his face, and breathed in until the anger came flooding back.

Instead of going home, he pulled into a diner, locked himself in a restroom stall, and slid the panties on. He masturbated quickly, then went back to the wooded lot, parked in the same place, and finished himself off again.

In 1953, at nineteen, Naso joined the US Air Force. He was already a rapist, but now he had a uniform, a symbol of authority that made women lower their guard. Throughout his four-year hitch, he was stationed around the country. Every new city was fresh hunting ground.

Before his service ended, he was written up for sexual assault. But nothing came of it. The military looked the other way. No charges, no investigation. Just silence. For Joe, that silence was permission.

He bragged to me, his eyes gleaming with pride: "By the time I left the Air Force, I'd taken sixteen women in the States and two overseas. You know what was best? Raping a broad in uniform. She thought she had power—until I forced her legs apart. Then she didn't have shit."

The Air Force hadn't stopped him. It had given him reach, confidence, and the belief he was untouchable. His military career was just a stepping stone, not the end.

Naso carried that sense of permission with him for decades. Twice—in 1955 and again in 1962—he was actually charged with sexual assault. But both cases collapsed when the victims refused to testify. Each time, he was quietly told to leave town.

Those failures only reinforced his belief that he was untouchable. In Naso's own words: "I raped 113 whores. They needed to be shown what they really were." In the next breath, though, he insisted, "I didn't rape anyone. They all wanted it and needed it."

And in that space between rape and impunity, evil was waiting.

14

Susan

Murder didn't announce itself all at once. It crept in, hidden inside Joe's obsessions, waiting for the night when opportunity and impulse finally collided. And when it did, he never forgot her.

One morning, he sat across from me, restless, studying my face as if weighing how much to share. Then, with a spark in his eyes, he leaned forward. "There's a girl in those magazines you got me who looks just like someone I photographed. She was my favorite of them all."

I nodded, careful not to press, encouraging him to go on. This was one he hadn't spoken of before—the girl who would open the door to something darker.

DATE: 1965
LOCATION: Richmond, California
NASO'S LIST: #1. The Girl near Heldsburg [sic], Mendocino Co. [Healdsburg, Sonoma County]
VICTIM: Susan [Lorraine]

Naso hadn't been in the Bay Area long. He'd uprooted his young family from Philadelphia, where he hadn't lived long either. But he'd pushed his luck with two rapes, and arrest felt close. So he moved again, west this time, close to his brother. Out of sight, out of mind.

Joseph Naso and his son. 1960s. Proud father, veteran rapist, and budding serial killer.

Except predators don't change zip codes—they change hunting grounds. In Richmond, at age thirty-one, Naso found two things: the cover of a new life and the first woman he would kill.

By then, he had built himself a front in photography, seeing it as his calling. With sample prints and flyers, he knocked on doors like a traveling salesman, pitching "family portraits in the comfort of your home." He was skilled enough to look legitimate, charming enough to be invited in. Mothers trusted him. Children smiled for his camera. And when the sessions were done, Joe drove away not thinking about exposure or lighting but about the women he'd watched and the ones he wanted.

One Friday afternoon, after photographing three children for a housewife in Richmond, he couldn't shake the girl he'd met weeks earlier at a bar nearby. Dark eyes. Shoulder-length hair. She had walked right up to him, all friendliness, and then spoiled the moment by asking if he wanted sex—for money.

He went along and took her to a small motel. But once he'd had her, the illusion shattered. He'd hoped she liked him for himself. Instead, she angled for cash, confirming what he already suspected.

"She looked like a nice chick," Joe told me. "But she was just another whore. A liar. I hated her from that moment."

The hatred didn't push her away. It bound him to her, fusing with the desire that already gnawed at him. For nearly a month, he watched her, tracked her routine, and counted the men. Each time, his anger rose—and so did his arousal. But killing her hadn't crossed his mind. Not yet.

The week before, he hooked up with her again, this time luring her to another motel under the pretense of his photography. She let him tie her up, and he snapped frame after frame, her bound body exactly as he wanted it.

That's when the thought turned real: the urge to strangle her while he was inside her. Until then, it had been a fantasy. But that night, he knew. The rush would come in the moment she died.

So he made plans. He drove the back roads of Sonoma County, scouting. Near the Del Rio Forest, he found the perfect spot to leave her: secluded but accessible. A place he could come back to, the way he revisited the places he'd raped before, reliving his conquest.

Now, that Friday, the girl named Susan would be his.

When he saw her outside the L & B Bar in North Richmond, he slowed his Chevy to the curb.

"Hi Joe! Looking for me?" She climbed in without hesitation.

"I sure am," he said, smiling. "Been thinking a lot about you."

"Oh yeah? Me too."

Joe heard the lie in her voice, and his hands tightened on the wheel. The steering column groaned under his grip.

She reached over and massaged his shoulder. "Relax, sugar. You're too tense."

He forced a smile. "I got us a place. Somewhere we can have some fun. Maybe take more pictures. Who knows—I might make you famous."

She laughed, pretending to like the idea. But when they drove past one motel after another, unease flickered across her face. "Where are we going, Joe? We've passed plenty of places."

Sorry," he said gently. "I've got equipment set up at a place not far. Clean walls. Good light. You'll see."

That calmed her. "So tell me about these pictures. How much?" The sweet nineteen-year-old turned all businesslike again.

"Nothing crazy. Some classy shots in lingerie. No nudes. I'll pay you double your normal rate. Sex lasts a few minutes, but pictures are forever."

"Triple," she said flatly.

Joe clenched his jaw. "Okay, but we sign a contract. I don't want anyone else discovering you."

The "contract" did it for her. Naso didn't care about the money. Besides, he wouldn't have to pay her a dime.

He pulled into the Marin Motel, parking in back where no one could see. Inside, the room looked legit—camera equipment staged, backdrops pinned up. Joe had staged the scene before, dozens of times. But that night, his hands trembled, a twitch of nerves he couldn't mask. She saw the crack beneath the charm and started edging toward the door.

"Joe, I don't want to do this after all."

That was the spark. He lunged, yanked her back by the hair, and smashed his fist into her face. She dropped, dazed. He tied her wrists to the bed, her arms spread, and then gagged her and ripped off her clothes.

The camera clicked, each frame steadying him. When she stirred and tears rolled down her cheeks, the sight thrilled him. The truth. He was in control, unstoppable.

He raped her and strangled her into unconsciousness again. When she came to, he did it again, repeating the cycle three times, savoring the slow build toward the moment he'd been imagining.

The last time, she tried moving with him, her hips rising to meet his. Maybe she thought it would placate him. Instead, it enraged him.

"She was trying to take my control," he told me.

So he locked his hands around her throat and didn't let go until her body gave out.

Afterward, he photographed the body. He showered and then untied her wrists, slid under the sheets beside her, and drifted off to sleep. Later, he woke and had sex with the corpse several times over the next few hours.

The next night, he wrapped her in a motel blanket and carried her to the trunk. He gathered all his camera equipment, her small purse, and her clothes and shoes. Inside the purse, he found eleven dollars and an ID.

She wasn't Susan.

Her name was Lorraine. She was eighteen years old.

Joe kept the panties, dumped the rest along Highway 101, and drove north toward Healdsburg. At a dirt turnoff near the Del Rio Forest, he continued for another mile and stopped.

He placed her over his shoulder and grabbed his flashlight, using it sparingly. It was a moonless night and he didn't want to fall. Near a small stream, he laid her in a thicket of trees.

But he didn't leave right away. He unwrapped her and masturbated over her one final time. It was difficult to tear himself away, though he knew there would be others.

When Joe finished telling me the story, he smiled faintly. "I've been chasing that rush ever since," he said. "I've gotten close—real close—but she was the best. I compare all of them to her."

"What about her was different?"

"I don't know. It was so intense, so perfect."

I thought back to his list. Naso knew the Bay Area well, but what he wrote was wrong: "Girl Near Heldsburg, Mendocino County." He not only misspelled Healdsburg but put it in the wrong county. When I pointed out the error, he waved me off.

"Close enough," he muttered.

He was done talking about the first girl he killed.

15

Leslie

Naso had a way of sensing when I was watching him. More than once, the instant I fixed my gaze, his head would snap around as if someone had tapped him on the shoulder.

That day was no different. He caught me staring and drifted over to the fence, smirking.

"Did you watch the Oakland A's game last night?" he asked. Before I could answer, he barreled on. "I used to know a lot of them. Back in the seventies, I'd get in with my press credentials."

This was something new. "I didn't know you were a reporter," I said.

"I wasn't. I said I had press credentials, not that I was a reporter." He chuckled. "Bought 'em off a forger—tools of the trade. They got me into places a ticket never could: dugouts, locker rooms, even celebrity events."

I let him talk, careful not to interrupt. More and more he seemed to be reliving his past and pulling me along for the ride.

"So, Joe," I finally asked, playing dumb, "why not just buy a ticket? Wouldn't that get you in the same way?"

"No, no." His eyes lit up. "The press pass got me on the field. Into the clubhouse. I knew Vida Blue, Rollie Fingers, Don Baylor—half the Raiders too. See a guy often enough, they figure you're legit."

He started to giggle, that thin, high-pitched sound I'd come to dread and despise. "Did I tell you how the Oakland A's even helped me get a girl?"

DATE: May 10, 1975
LOCATION: Oakland, California
NASO'S LIST: #4. The Girl on Mt. Tam
VICTIM: Leslie

It was game two of the three-day series between the Oakland A's and the New York Yankees.

That Saturday, Joe pulled into the Coliseum lot hours before first pitch. Only a few cars dotted the asphalt, the stadium looming above. At the players' entrance, he flashed his fake press credentials. The guard waved him through without a glance.

For Joe, this was a thrill. On the field and in the locker room, the players treated him like he belonged. He blended in so easily—just another face with a badge around his neck. No one suspected the smiling photographer collecting autographs was a serial killer, primed for violence.

That day, though, he wasn't prowling. He was a fan brushing shoulders with the stars he'd idolized as a boy.

Until he saw her.

Near the visiting dugout stood a redhead in bell-bottoms and a tied blouse, a rabbit-fur purse hanging from her arm. The Indian choker at her throat caught his eye—and so did the way she looked at him. Not a smile, but a half-daring, half-vulnerable stare.

His jaw tightened. He raised the camera and snapped her picture. Click. Then another.

He climbed toward her in the stands and handed her a business card. Not glancing at it, she shifted her weight and let him take more shots.

Her blue eyes and body language spoke louder than words. Naso read it the way he always did. Invitation. Manipulation. Sex. And already the monster stirred.

"How's it going?" he said, his voice casual. "I'm Joe, the A's photographer. I think your look could open a lot of doors for you."

She crossed her arms, pressing her breasts together. "Yeah?" The throaty laugh that followed confused him. Was she teasing him? Mocking him? Maybe she was high.

A heat rose in him, sharp and unwelcome. He hated the loss of control it stirred. And he hated her. In his mind, he was already at her throat, squeezing until the laughter stopped.

Taking a deep breath, he caught himself. Focus. First, he needed to isolate her. "Have you modeled before?"

She shrugged. "Maybe. Kinda." Another laugh.

He baited the hook. "I'd like to shoot you for my next exhibit. Did you come with your boyfriend? If he doesn't mind, we can start right away. Standard modeling fees. Say, $125?"

"I didn't come with anyone," she said quickly. "Took the bus. I like baseball and the players."

Perfect. Alone.

"Let me buy you a beer. Think it over."

At the concession stand, Naso sealed the illusion. "Hi, Debra, two beers," he told the girl behind the counter as if they were old friends.

She smiled back, playing along without knowing it, reinforcing his cover. "Hi, Joe. Sure thing. What're you up to today?"

Naso flashed a wad of bills. "I just finished the player profiles, and we're about to do a fan appreciation day, so I'm busy, busy," he said.

He handed the redhead her beer. "You never told me your name."

"Leslie."

"I'm Joe. It's on the card I gave you."

She slid his card from her blouse—no bra beneath—and arched an eyebrow. Professional photographer, Oakland Athletics. She looked impressed.

Naso felt the charge of it. People believed what they saw. They always had.

"So how do we do this?" she asked. "Go to a studio? That'd be hot."

"Not for this project—it needs to be on location. The series is called *Beauty in Nature*. Streams, redwoods, meadows. You in the middle of it. That's the vision."

She grinned. "Cool. I'll go for it. When and where?"

Naso's pulse quickened. "How about today? I'll pay travel time too. Four hours max."

She hesitated, her eyes drifting to the field as the teams ran out.

Naso leaned in smoothly. "The Yankees will be here again tomorrow. I'll leave a pass for you at the gate. Maybe I'll even introduce you to some of the players."

Her face lit up. "Wow. Okay. I'll do it."

She had no idea the danger she'd stepped into.

No one noticed the pretty redhead leave with the middle-aged man, not with the game starting and the stadium alive.

Naso knew exactly where he was taking her. He'd scouted the place weeks earlier—a secluded stretch near Mount Tamalpais, the "Sleeping Lady." Perfect for what he intended.

They drove north on Highway 1, the coastline glimmering in the afternoon light, and then headed east near Stinson Beach. As they twisted through mountain roads, she talked. Twenty-two years old, kicked out by her parents at sixteen when she got pregnant, she said. Abortion, odd jobs, crashing with friends. "I'm just doing my thing," she told him between drags on a joint.

She was lying. He was convinced. And when she let slip she'd taken money for sex, the monster inside him snapped awake. To him, she'd just confirmed it—another whore, another liar in need of "cleaning."

Close to West Peak, Naso found the turnoff. He parked on the side of the dirt road and pulled a camera case, nylon bag, and gray blanket from the trunk.

"Let's go past those trees," he said, pointing toward a meadow bathed in soft light. "It's beautiful there."

The shoot began with harmless poses: leaning against a tree, sitting on a rock, shadows playing across her face. She played along easily, almost enjoying it. When he suggested lingerie, she stripped without hesitation and pulled on the pieces he'd brought. They fit perfectly. Her creamy white skin, freckles, the scar near her belly button—he stared at it all, camera shutter clicking, his arousal impossible to hide.

"Take the stockings off," he told her. When she obeyed, he used one to bind her wrists and the other to loop around her throat. "Pretend you're terrified. Captive."

She played the part. That thrilled him more than her nakedness.

When Naso dropped the camera down and knelt beside her, she unbuckled his pants with bound hands and put him in her mouth. To him, it was theft—stealing his control. Rage poured through him. He let her continue, then shoved her back on the blanket and forced himself into her. She began to move with him, trying to turn submission into survival, but he saw only defiance. She was taking his power back.

"Fuckin' whore," he growled, his hands clamping around her throat. "Fuckin' red whore."

He shook her violently, tightening his grip as he thrust, each squeeze an answer to her imagined deception. Her struggles weakened. He came as her body went limp.

For a long time, he lay across her, unmoving. When he finally rolled away, he dozed beside her until the sun had sunk behind the trees.

In the fading light, he posed her—hands still bound, body now slack in death—and took more photos. Smoking one of her joints, he pawed through her rabbit-fur purse: makeup, eighteen dollars, photo-booth strips, a Yankees pin, some rolling papers. Souvenirs.

Over the next hour, he raped her corpse twice before gathering her things and lingerie into his bag, carrying the blanket back to the car, and returning for the body. Lifting her easily, he carried her to a ravine near the meadow and left her in the shadows.

He drove away in the dark, content.

On the radio, the Doors' *Riders on the Storm* came on. The rain, the organ, Morrison's voice murmuring about a killer on the road. It was as if the music had been made for him. Soon after, he bought the cassette, and it became part of the ritual: the song he wanted playing whenever he was dumping a body—or driving away after leaving one behind.

When I asked Joe why he chose that location, he told me how the Sleeping Lady and Mount Tamalpais reminded him of Camelot, the Lady of the Lake, and King Arthur. He even referred to a location close to where he'd left her: Arturo Trail next to West Peak.

He laughed. "I'm the king."

For a moment he hummed softly. Then he stopped, his eyes flicking up at me.

"You know, Bill, I left more than one girl on Mount Tam."

16

The Second Girl

He didn't finish the story then. It came later, while he was talking about so-called rest periods.

"The cops are idiots," he said. "They think they know when I stopped and when I started up again. They don't know shit."

He turned around in his chair and smirked up at me. "They even found some of mine but were too stupid to connect them. They blamed Rodney Alcala instead."

At the mention of Alcala's name, I stopped pushing him.

The Dating Game Killer. He'd actually appeared on the '70s TV show *The Dating Game*—and won. He never went on the date, though. The bachelorette took one look at him backstage and refused, saying he gave her the creeps. Alcala was a photographer too, prowling the same streets as Naso then, camera slung over his shoulder as his lure. And like Naso, he'd left behind a trail of women. He was sitting just across the wall from us on yard four, protective custody.

"What do you mean they blamed it on him?" I asked.

"I met this broad at an A's game in '77. Blonde, pretty, real nice. Said she was dating one of the players. We agreed to meet up at Fisherman's Wharf."

His face twisted in delight. "She kept going on about being an entertainer, about how these photos would make her a star. What a motor mouth. Drove me crazy. So I made sure she was entertaining all right."

> *Naso made a mistake today. He reveals details I don't believe he intended. He gets caught up in the moment. Today he spoke about Rodney Alcala again. He seems very pleased that Rodney was blamed for one his murders. He said he put (2) girls on Mount Tam. (1970s) One of them was girl he picked up at Fishers w). who Alcala was blamed for. (He mentioned posing one of them as a joke.) - Naso mixes up names. The stories stay consistant, but names he changes or forgets. Said he left up against tree.*

My journal: Naso told me he left two girls on Mount Tam, one blamed on Alcala.

He giggled—that same sick noise that scraped at me. I had to fight the urge to silence him with my fists.

"How so?" I asked.

"I posed her against a tree on Mount Tam. But the dumb cops blamed Alcala."

At the time, I didn't know her name. Joe wouldn't give it to me. Just another girl discarded on the mountain.

Later, I spoke to Alcala himself through the fence. I asked him directly about the girl on Mount Tam. He vehemently denied killing her or even having any contact with her. He'd gone so far as to write letters to law enforcement denying his involvement—something he had never done before.

And yet, Alcala admitted to other murders without hesitation. He told me about Robin Samsoe, Jill Barcomb, Charlotte Lamb, and several others, even showing me photographs and recounting their stories. But when it came to the girl on Mount Tam, he was unwavering. He didn't do it.

Now Naso was claiming her as his, pleased to be setting the record straight in his own twisted way.

Naso's photography permit for Alameda County, California. 1977–1978.

17

Girl from Berkeley

He was always hunting, always looking for the right girl. In a bar, at a ballgame, or walking down the street—he scanned faces, watching for the smallest opening.

Some serial killers stick to a type—joggers, hitchhikers, prostitutes. Naso wasn't that narrow. His type was opportunity.

That didn't mean he was careless. The FBI would have called him an "organized killer": one who plans, rehearses, and refines his method, sometimes for years. He stalks his victims, fantasizes about his crimes, and studies the aftermath in the news. Naso was all of that.

But he could also strike without warning. That was his edge: patience one night, sudden violence the next.

The girl from Berkeley was one of those moments. And when he first told me about her, I had no idea how significant her story would become.

DATE: May 19–20, 1976
LOCATION: Oakland, California
NASO'S LIST: #6. The Girl from Berkeley
VICTIM: Unknown

Joe sat alone at his kitchen table, sipping coffee. Judith and his young sons had left that morning and wouldn't be back until the following evening.

A week earlier, he'd spotted an ad in the *Berkeley Barb*, the underground paper. A young woman was looking for work as a nude model "for artists or art classes." No photo or details, just a phone number.

Now, with the house to himself, he dialed.

A woman answered on the third ring.

"Yes, hi," Joe said. "I'm calling about the ad."

"One moment, please."

He heard muffled voices in the background before another voice came on—lighter, younger. "Hello?"

"Good morning. My name is Jeff," he lied smoothly. "I'm a professional photographer here in the Bay Area. I'm looking for new talent. Would you like to meet?"

"Yes, absolutely. I'd need to ride my bike, though, so we have to pick a place close by."

Joe stiffened. "Your bike? How old are you?"

She laughed. "I'm twenty. I just don't drive. I prefer my bike."

He exhaled. "Good. You had me worried there for a second. Where can we meet?"

"I'm in Berkeley. Do you know the area?"

"Of course. I've shot there before."

"Perfect. There's a restaurant on Telegraph, Bateau Ivre. We could meet there."

"I know the place. Tomorrow morning? I'm on deadline and need to move fast."

"How about around 10:30?"

"Works for me," he said.

The next morning, Joe rose at six. He wasn't in a hurry. He arranged his lighting, prepped his cameras, and laid out lingerie. He wanted everything ready. By 9:30, he was on the road, savoring the anticipation.

To him, a nude model was no different from a prostitute—someone willing to sell her body. Women like that were all whores, art or not. The thought made him hard. He didn't need to see her to know what he wanted.

He parked across from Bateau Ivre just after ten, watching until she appeared. Moments later, she rode up on a bicycle, locked it, and slipped inside. Joe walked to the restaurant door—and almost at once, as if pulled by a magnet, the girl came back out and spotted him.

She smiled. "Jeff?"

"Yes." He nodded and reached into his pocket for his card: "Jeff Napoli, Professional Photographer."

She had a beautiful body, hidden under black Levis and a T-shirt. But what struck Joe most was her face. She looked like his mother.

"So what do you think?" she asked, her arms slightly turned out in a shy attempt at a pose. "Do I look like what you might need for the shoot?" She smiled again.

He studied her, the perfect Berkeley girl, mid-'70s, all youth and idealism and soft talk of love and kindness. But then a memory intruded—his mother's voice and her breathless moan in bed with the neighbor. *Choke me.*

"Yes," he said to the girl. "I believe you do. What are your rates? And are you available now?"

"Cool." She bit her lip. "Well, I normally charge forty for full-body nudes, twenty-five for topless." Her voice dropped to a whisper. "But if you need something else, I'd be happy to give you a quote."

Her words set his skin on fire. He'd been right—another whore in disguise. All lies. Her innocent act stoked his hatred even as it aroused him.

"Let's agree on full-body nudes," he said. "We'll see where that takes us. I've got another shoot later today, so let's head on over to my studio."

"Yeah?" she said, once again playing the vulnerable young girl act.

She left her bike chained to the bike rack, leaving behind the only trace she was ever there.

━━━

They drove back to Oakland, the ride just long enough for Joe to slip into the quiet space where the killer waited, preparing to strike at the right moment.

At the house he shared with his wife and sons, the girl asked, almost casually, if she could use the bathroom.

"Down the hall, first door on the left," Joe said. "I'll set up."

He watched her walk away, jaw clenched so tight it ached. Hatred pulsed just beneath the surface. Everything about her—her youth, her pose, her uncanny resemblance to his mother—stoked the old rage. Yes, she needed to be cleaned.

When she emerged, she looked effortless: blond hair spilling around her face, flat stomach curving into the flare of her hips. Joe stared at her like a spider fixed on a fly. She bit her lip, turned her feet inward—playing the vulnerable sex kitten. His hand trembled between anticipation and fury.

His camera steadied him. Click. "Beautiful," he said. "Now walk toward me."

She followed his instructions, stretching out on the couch as he snapped frame after frame. Normally, he obsessed over lighting, but now he barely cared. Each shot conjured a ghost—his mother on her knees with the neighbor.

The words left his mouth before he realized: "Choke me."

Startled, the girl started to sit up and then caught sight of the bulge in his pants. He softened his tone. "It's all right."

As she relaxed back into the cushions, he set the camera down and stroked her hair gently, over and over. Then, with sudden force, his hands clamped around her throat, pinning her beneath his weight.

She fought hard—twisting, clawing, refusing to yield. For a moment, she held her own. But his strength and cold resolved crushed her. Her movements slowed. Her eyes dimmed. And then she went still.

Breathless, Joe heaved himself off her, smoothed his thinning hair, and calmly lifted his Nikon again. He photographed her still form, capturing what he sought. The truth.

Sated but restless, he stripped and leaned her against him, pretending intimacy. She felt warm. Overwhelmed with hatred once again, he stood over her and masturbated, muttering under his breath.

A shower washed the sweat from his body, but not the image from his mind. His wife and sons weren't due back until evening, but the thought of them walking in pushed him back to the kitchen, dripping, naked. He made coffee, checked the clock—2:30. Hours to spare.

Sitting at the kitchen table, he relived moments from his life: the first time he put on his mother's underwear, the day he saw her having sex, the first time he killed someone, and, finally, the girl from Berkeley, who was still on his couch in his living room.

Hours slipped by. When he came to, the house was dark. The clock read 8:15. Panic jolted him upright. His family could be home any second.

He rushed into the bathroom to gather the girl's things, stuffing them into a camera case. Levi's. Shirt. No underwear. "Fuckin' whore."

Back in the living room, he yanked his clothes on, fumbling with the buttons, his ears straining for the sound of tires on the drive. Then he rolled the girl up in a blanket, tied it off with rope, and hauled her over his shoulder to the trunk of his Chevy.

As the lid slammed, headlights swept across the driveway—Judith and the boys.

Instantly, the killer vanished. The husband and father stepped forward. He kissed his wife, carried groceries inside, and let his children climb on him, laughing. No one would imagine there was a dead girl hidden in his trunk.

Later that night, after Judith was sound asleep, he slipped out. At 2:35 a.m., he eased the car onto the quiet street and drove to the Richmond–San Rafael Bridge, a half hour from his house.

It was deserted. Just the sweep of steel and the dark water below. No security cameras. No cell phones. This was a time when people, especially women, went missing, never to be heard from again. Good for serial killers. Not so good for their victims.

He opened the trunk, hefted the bundled body onto his shoulder, and walked to the railing. To anyone watching, it would look like he was carrying a rolled carpet. He tipped it over. Seconds later, he heard the splash, then silence.

A good day's work.

Back home, he slid into bed. By morning, no one would even know she'd existed.

When I asked Joe her name, he shrugged. "I don't know. Too many girls—it's hard to remember all of them by name."

Maybe age blurred his memory, but ask him about a football player from 1962, and he'd rattle off stats with perfect recall. He remembered what mattered to him.

For Naso, names meant nothing. Women weren't people. They were prey, bodies to be posed, erased, forgotten. That was the only truth he cared to preserve.

And yet, when he told their stories—whether once or a dozen times—the details rarely changed. The consistency was chilling, as if the murders were etched into him more indelibly than the names of the women he took.

18

The Call

While Naso replayed his past in fragments and boasts, I was trapped in a different kind of story—one with an ending still unwritten. I didn't know it yet, but the call that night would change everything.

November 17, 2017. 6:51 p.m. The fourth-tier phone cart rattled to a stop in front of my cell.

"Phone tonight, Mr. Noguera," the older guard said.

"Yes, please," I said.

I reached through the food port, took the receiver, and dialed Tina. More than three decades had passed since we'd been teenagers together at La Habra High, but she still treated me like a friend, not a condemned prisoner. Her warmth was a lifeline I didn't deserve but held onto anyway.

She answered on the third ring. "Hi, gorgeous," I said, like always.

"Hi yourself, handsome."

A hesitation in her voice caught me. "You doing okay?"

"Better now. Can I read you something?"

"Of course."

Her words started like a poem—about the boy I'd once been, the friend she remembered. Then her tone shifted.

"It is the decision of this court, that the petitioner, William A. Noguera, did not receive a fair trial. . . . The judgment of death is vacated, and the conviction of first-degree murder is overturned. The

State of California has one hundred and twenty days to retry the case, or release the prisoner."

For a second, I thought she was imagining again—projecting like she often did. Then silence stretched.

"Wait," I said. "Where are you reading that from?"

"I'm reading the court's order. I got a call this afternoon. The court reversed your conviction. You're coming home."

I sat frozen, the phone pressed to my ear, staring at the steel and concrete walls that had defined my life for thirty-five Christmases. After years of appeals, stays of execution, and hearings, a federal judge finally heard my case. For the first time since 1983, I was just Bill—not a condemned prisoner, not an inmate number. Bill.

But prison never lets you breathe for long.

Four months later, the California Attorney General appealed to the Ninth Circuit, tossing me back into limbo. Legal purgatory. Freedom dangled in front of me, then yanked away again.

And all the while, on the ADA yard, Joseph Naso shuffled beside me, smelling of decay, teeth rotting, body failing, but still clutching his secrets. My window with him could be closing. If the courts pulled me out before I finished—before I had something solid enough to hand over—everything I'd risked would be for nothing.

So I lived in two timelines at once: the one in the courts, where lawyers and judges debated my fate, and the one in the yard, where a serial killer's confessions slipped out between muttered slurs and sick giggles.

Both lives converged in me. And neither would let me go.

19

Carmen: The Street

Joe seldom launched straight into a confession. He treated each story like a performance, setting the stage before letting me in. With cops or reporters, he clammed up—they were the enemy, the ones who could charge him with additional crimes. Why would he tell them anything?

With me, he thought he had an audience. Sometimes he would stop opening up, not sure he could still trust me. But sooner or later, he'd circle back. The ghosts of his past were never far, and sooner or later the urge to share them returned.

I needed breaks too. What he gave me came raw—humiliating, twisted, stripped of disguise. Because he believed I wouldn't run to law enforcement, he offered glimpses no detective ever got. But the weight of those stories drained me, leaving me hollow, forcing me to claw back at some shred of my own humanity.

Serial killers are rare, wired differently, shaped by forces most people will never know. Joe knew it too. That's why each revelation felt dangerous, as if he was dragging me into a world only he could describe.

And what he shared next pulled me deeper still—into the compulsions that defined him.

DATE: July 21, 1978
LOCATION: Oakland, California
NASO'S LIST: #2. The Girl near Port Costa
VICTIM: Carmen Colon
Part One: The Street

Joe slammed the door behind him, still fuming from the morning's fight. Sixteen years with Judith, and now it was constant nagging. She hated his photography, hated the women he brought around, and, most of all, hated that he wouldn't admit what she already knew—that the models were really prostitutes. More than once, she'd screamed at him for finding their bed in a state of disarray, the sheets reeking of another woman.

The night before, Judith's suspicions had been paraded in public. At the mall, two hookers called out, "Hey Joe, come see us soon, sugar! Don't forget about us!" Right in front of his wife and kids. Judith's face burned with humiliation. Joe, meanwhile, soaked up the attention.

Back home, she told him to sleep elsewhere, her eyes filled with tears. By morning, the fight had only escalated, and when he returned home, it continued.

"Why, Joe?" she said, not letting him look away.

"I'm tired. I just want to sleep."

"Then sleep. But not in my bed."

For a moment, he considered killing her. He'd imagined it before. But she was the mother of his sons—that was the only thing that stopped him.

So he drove toward his secret Oakland studio on Market Street. No phone, no records, cash only. A place where Judith couldn't find him, and he could do whatever he pleased. If he needed to make a call, he walked across the street to the pay phone. Simple. That's how Joe liked it.

Still seething, he pulled into a liquor store on San Pablo and MacArthur. Inside, he grabbed two cranberry juices, then pocketed gum and mints on his way to the counter.

"That all?" the clerk asked.

"Yeah," Joe muttered, tossing down some bills.

"Come again."

Joe went back into the night, the small thrill of theft easing his rage. Distracted, he almost walked straight into the young woman leaning against his car, smiling like she'd been waiting.

"Hey, honey, looking for a date tonight?"

Joe looked her over. "Maybe. That depends."

"On what, hon? Let Mama take care of you." She pressed herself against him.

"What's your name?"

"Carmen," she said, sliding her hand over his crotch.

He reached for her large breasts and kissed her neck. "How much?"

"I'll suck you dry for twenty. Fuck you good for thirty."

Before he could answer, she slipped into the car. By the time he closed his door, she already had his zipper down. "Too many lights here," she said, stroking him. "Let's go somewhere dark."

Her control both aroused and enraged him. Whores were supposed to be beneath him, but here she was, dictating everything. The monster stirred.

He drove them to an area off San Pablo, into the empty, shadowed lots. Before he even stopped, she took him into her mouth.

"That's right, bitch," he growled, forcing her head down. "Take it all."

But no matter how he tried, she stayed in control. When he used his trump card—his weapon to define all women—and thrust himself into her spread legs, she once again took control, arching back against him, setting the rhythm, mocking his dominance.

"Fuckin' animal!" she cried out.

Confusion, arousal, fury—all twisted inside him. She unsettled him in a way that made him want her gone. And yet she fascinated him.

Later, he dropped her off at the liquor store. He was about to say "See you around," when she leaned back through the window with a smirk. "Don't be a stranger, honey. I'll be waiting."

Even the final word she stole from him.

At his studio, his wrath erupted. He hurled a mannequin to the floor, straddled it, and wrapped his hands around its throat.

"Fuckin' whore cunt. Just like the rest of 'em. I'm gonna kill you, fuck you, kill you again. Die, bitch, die."

The violence vanished as quickly as it came. Joe faced his reflection in the mirror—the same mirror he'd had in the apartment where he killed Roxene Roggasch.

He whispered to himself, "What do you say, Joe? Do we kill the big-tit whore?"

"Oh, yes. Fuck her, kill her, clean her."

From that night on, Joe prepared. Patient and unseen, he tracked her movements through his long lens, from car to car, from john to john, into back alleys and darkened lots. Each time, his anger grew.

And each time, death moved one step closer.

20

Carmen: The Studio

DATE: August 5, 1978
LOCATION: Oakland, California
NASO'S LIST: #2. The Girl near Port Costa
VICTIM: Carmen Colon
Part Two: The Studio

After two weeks, Joe no longer needed to stalk from a distance. Carmen was right there, under the glow of the barbershop pole. She was ripe for his lens, ripe for his hands. The waiting was over.

That warm night, he spotted her by the closed shop, the light above her head making her look almost staged—like a subject already framed for him. His stomach clenched.

She leaned into his window the moment he pulled to the curb. "Hi, papi, you come back for some of this?" She tugged her top down, exposing her ample breasts.

Christ, she was doing it again, always taking control. Tonight he'd take that control forever.

"Sure," Joe said evenly. "Get in."

Carmen jumped into the passenger seat and ran her hand up his thigh. "Damn, papi, looks like someone missed me. Where we going?"

"My place. I'll pay you extra to stay awhile. Maybe pose for me."

"Are you a painter?"

"No," he said with pride. "A professional photographer. An artist. You'll be the focus of my work." He gave her a thin smile. "I promise you'll never be forgotten."

At his studio, she walked in first. To her, it might have looked like a shabby apartment cluttered with dishes and equipment. To Joe, it was a temple. His cameras. His lights. And his mannequins—five of them in different wigs and lingerie, frozen in poses only he understood. One was bound and gagged, a pair of pantyhose wrapped around its neck.

"This is where I capture the truth life," he said, camera in hand. "No masks. No lies. My lens reveals everything."

Her eyes darted from the mannequins to the camera. The confidence she'd worn outside faltered. Good. The streetwise whore was slipping, and in her place, he saw what she really was—an insecure girl. He fed on it.

"Let's start slow," he said. "Natural poses. Just you."

He sat her on the couch and gave her props: a phone receiver, then a book. Each click of the shutter drew her deeper in. The light, the angles, his voice guiding her—it all lulled her. She laughed once, as if it was fun. Nails on glass to him.

Joe set the camera down. "I picked out a gorgeous outfit for you." He handed her a small box. "Wear this."

Inside: black-and-red lingerie. Carmen disappeared into the bathroom and came back as he'd imagined—corset tight, garters framing her thighs, breasts straining against lace. He snapped shot after shot, the camera punctuating his breath.

She preened at the mirror and smiled.

"Lovely," Joe said.

When he turned to pick up another camera, she leaned into him, rubbing his erection. "Come on, Daddy," she purred, "make me yours."

His fury ignited. He shoved her onto the couch and drove into her from behind. But she took over, moving hard against him, setting the rhythm, speaking the words. She dared to control him at the edge of his climax.

He slammed her to the floor onto her back and entered her again, one hand already reaching for a stocking to loop around her throat.

Then she said it.

"Choke me."

The words ripped him back decades, to his mother moaning the same to the neighbor. A white-hot rage consumed him.

"Die, whore!" he screamed, yanking the stocking tight.

Carmen jolted upward, clawing at his hands, but he only pulled harder and harder—until her body sagged beneath him.

Joe held fast, savoring the silence. At last, he let the stocking fall.

"Perfect," he whispered. "Now you're clean."

He photographed her where she lay. Then he carried her to the bedroom, arranged her on the bed, and kept shooting. The sight of her lifeless body stirred him again, hotter than before.

It was natural to him, what came next. Girls unconscious, girls dead—it didn't matter. Dead was better. Dead was pure.

Afterward, at peace, he stood before the mirror, naked, arms spread. "So many girls, so little time."

He couldn't stop laughing as he stepped into the hot spray of the shower.

When Joe finally emerged, the air was thick with steam. He dried off slowly and got dressed—pants, shirt, shoes—as though nothing had happened.

"Time to take out the trash," he said.

He cut a strand of Carmen's hair, tied it with red ribbon, and tucked it with her panties into a small wooden chest, where he kept special items from his girls. The rest of her clothes went in a paper bag.

At 2:15 a.m., Joe carried her body to the trunk of his car and tossed her things onto the passenger-side floor. Pulling onto I-80, he drove east toward the town of Crockett near Port Costa, where cattle ranches stretched across the landscape and solitude still ruled the open fields. The perfect place to dump a body.

Close to 3 a.m., Joe pulled over and cut the engine, leaving himself in absolute darkness. The silence was complete, broken only by his own steady breath and the hum of insects.

As he strained to get the dead girl out of his trunk, he dropped her on the road. "Goddammit, you're heavy," he muttered.

He hauled her to a patch of weeds and brush. Before leaving her, he scooped a handful of dirt from where she lay into a small plastic bag. "Enjoy your dirt nap, whore."

On the way back, he dumped her things in a public trash can, keeping only her ID. The rest was gone.

But Carmen would live forever in his collection.

21

Rebecca

In April 1979, *The Professional Photographer* magazine ran a feature on Naso titled "Portable Portraiture." The piece showcased his technique and praised his ability to turn ordinary portraits into art. For Joe, it was a breakthrough—his first real taste of what he craved most: recognition.

Flush with attention, he printed new business cards, bought a car, and finally separated from Judith. They hadn't shared a bed in far too long, and his resentment toward her had only deepened. Divorce was inevitable, but Joe hardly cared. In his mind, he had outgrown her. He was an artist now—too important for a wife who never understood him or his work.

The timing couldn't have been better. He began traveling often between the Bay Area and Las Vegas, intoxicated by the Strip's lights and the illusion that the entire city was applauding his arrival. He flashed copies of the magazine article like trophies, proof that he wasn't just another man with a camera—he was someone. A name.

But Las Vegas was more than a business opportunity. For Joe, it was a jewel in the desert—a fresh hunting ground where no one would suspect him.

Unlike many serial rapists and killers, Joe wasn't a "spree" predator. He didn't need to strike every week, or even every month. And he wasn't confined to a single area. The Bay Area, Nevada, other

THE PROFESSIONAL

Photographer. Apr. '79/

vol. 106 no. 2003

April 1979 issue of *The Professional Photographer* magazine featuring Naso.

states—each offered him opportunities, each a separate stage for his violence.

Over countless conversations on the yard, Joe boasted about the sheer number of rapes and murders that had never been tied to him. And he never missed a chance to sneer at the cops: "Lazy or just stupid. Took them sixty years to catch me, and even then, it was dumb luck. And they still got most of it wrong."

He was right about that much. Officially, he was convicted of killing four women and linked to two more. Yet his handwritten List of Ten still left four names unresolved—four women whose families never got answers.

What makes it worse is how simple it could have been. Investigators kept dragging Joe out for interviews while the real evidence sat untouched in his cell. His diary chronicled the past—his crimes, his victims, his kills—written so he could relive them. He showed it to me more than once, even on the yard. When the chance came, I stole pieces of it. Over time, I took several entries.

And then there were the photographs, hundreds of them. Women he posed, women he stalked, women who never walked away.

His diary and photographs revealed the darker truth: Joseph Naso never stopped returning to his crimes. He needed them. They sustained him. And in those pages and images—concealed in the ordinary—were confessions law enforcement never pried loose.

DATE: April–May 1979
LOCATION: Las Vegas, Nevada
NASO'S LIST: Not included
VICTIM: Rebecca (Becca)

It didn't take Joe long to spot her. She always worked her corner near the Riviera, where he'd picked her up last month. She had been on his mind ever since.

He pulled to the curb, and Rebecca—Becca, as he called her—

stepped toward him. Round face, blond hair, green eyes, and the kind of body that drew attention on the Strip. She bent down to the passenger window, giving the same tired line he'd heard a hundred times. "Hi, sugar." Then she recognized him. Oh, Joe. Haven't seen you in a while. Where ya been?"

He smiled, brimming with confidence. "Been busy. Interviews. Television appearances."

When she climbed in beside him, he shoved the glossy magazine into her hands. "Go on—see for yourself. They're writing about me now."

She glanced at the pages and then back at him with a half-smile. "Not bad, Joe. Guess I'm riding with a celebrity."

He loved the way she said it. He'd seen it before—the shift in their eyes when the magazine did its work. In her mind, a man in print meant money. And if he was famous, he had to be safe. Famous men didn't hurt girls. That was the hook. That's why he carried the article everywhere, ready to flash it like a badge.

"I almost didn't recognize you," she said. "New car?"

"New car, new life. Everything's moving up." He leaned closer, lowering his voice. "I've got an art exhibit coming up in Los Angeles. I want you in it—your name on the program and extra pay for posing."

That got her attention. She perked up, exactly as he expected.

But then her face clouded. "You know my friend—the Black girl who worked this spot with me? A few weeks ago, she got into some guy's car. Nobody's seen her since."

Joe kept his face still, but he chuckled inside. He remembered her well. Rebecca didn't know that the man sitting next to her had already taken her friend. *Two for the price of one*, he thought, as he softened his expression and gave her the slow, reassuring nod that always worked.

"How long will the pictures take?" she asked.

"About two hours. My studio's nearby. I'll pay you two hundred. Fair?"

The price was more than fair. Still, she stalled like they all did when they thought they had leverage. At last, she smiled. "Deal. What kind of pictures?"

"Role-playing. Lingerie. Close-ups."

She turned away, and he knew she wasn't pleased.

"What is it? Something I said?"

She shook her head. "No, Joe." A pause. "It just reminded me of something. When you said 'art exhibit,' it took me back to art school. Feels like a lifetime ago. I wanted to be an artist. That was my dream since I was a kid."

"Why'd you stop?"

She gave a small shrug. "Couldn't afford to keep going. Otherwise, I'd probably be showing my art in New York by now."

Joe's hands tightened on the wheel. *New York.* The arrogance. Comparing herself to him—as if she could be his equal. She was a whore, nothing else. He was the artist. He had vision. He had skill. She had nothing but a mouth to run and a body to sell.

By the time he pulled into the carport, rage burned under his skin. He wanted to kill her right then, before another word left her mouth. For a moment he considered skipping the photographs altogether—but he knew he'd regret it.

Inside the apartment, the mannequins in lingerie stood waiting, staged around the room. Cameras, lights, and backdrops crowded the space.

Joe handed her a box. "Try these on. Bathroom's right there. I'll set up for the shoot."

When she returned in teal and black lace, his breath caught. A vision. The color made her green eyes blaze under the lights, sharper, brighter, impossible to ignore. He raised his camera and began snapping. "Look at me. Walk toward me. Seduce the lens. Yes, that's it."

Shot after shot, until he had what he wanted. Almost.

"Now take off your panties and stockings," he said. "Kneel and look up at me."

She obeyed. Always.

He set the camera down and unbuckled his pants. She knew what came next and went through the motions. He barely noticed—he was already planning the final pose.

When he pulled her into the bedroom, she followed automatically, moving on instinct. And when he looped the stockings around her throat, she didn't resist at first—her eyes steady, as if it was just another trick of the trade. Then he yanked them tight. Her eyes snapped wide, the sudden flare of panic he lived for.

She bucked, clawing and gasping. He held fast, feeding on the moment as the fight drained out of her. Breathless. Still.

Now she was perfect. Pure. No more lies.

He picked up the camera again and clicked away, capturing the truth as only he could see it.

After a long, hot shower, Joe ate a roast beef TV dinner with mashed potatoes and corn and drank a beer.

Hours later, he stripped her bare, separating what he wanted to keep from what he would discard. Then he wrapped her body in plastic and tape, bagged up the rest of her things, and hauled it all out to the trunk.

By nearly three in the morning, Vegas had finally gone quiet. He pulled onto Fremont Street and soon merged onto I-15 heading south. Half an hour later, he took an exit and turned onto a small dirt road he'd scouted before. The ride was rough, the tires bumping over ruts for a couple of miles until he killed the lights and stopped. Under the stars, he dragged her from the trunk, carried her a short distance, and left her there in the desert night.

Driving back, he began to giggle, high and mocking, the sound bouncing in the empty car. In a falsetto voice, he mimicked her, "I'd probably be showing my art in New York . . ."

Then his own voice, sharp and cold: "Now you're exhibiting in the desert. Fuckin' whore. You all have stories of who you could have been. But I know who you really are."

22

Judith

By 1980, Joe was no longer living with his wife and sons. Judith had filed for divorce, and though he no longer loved her, the papers cut him to the core. For Joe, it was never about love—it was about possession and control. He obsessed over the idea that another man might take his place and have sex with her. The thought disgusted him and perversely aroused him.

He told me more than once that he wanted to watch Judith with another man, photograph her, and then kill her. "It turns me on to imagine Judith getting fucked," he said. "Choking her to death would do it for me."

Yet, when pressed, he always said the same thing: "She's the mother of my sons. I could never kill her." Amid all his contempt for women, that was the one line he clung to as proof of his humanity. He even had a soft spot for his son Charles, who struggled with schizophrenia and violent outbursts. His children were extensions of himself, and through them, he spared Judith.

But sparing her didn't mean he trusted her. In his warped logic, all women were deceitful and therefore deserved punishment. That belief went back to his earliest memory: catching his mother with a neighbor, and through a child's eyes, interpreting sex as betrayal. He never outgrew it. Instead, he built a twisted framework around it: women were in control, women were whores, women needed to be "exposed."

Even Judith.

So he devised a plan to prove himself right.

One night in San Francisco, after dinner and dancing, he slipped a "red devil"—the forerunner of today's roofies—into Judith's cocktail. He'd used it before on victims to make them "manageable" and less likely to draw attention. When the drug took hold, he steered her upstairs, supporting her weight as he pulled into a hotel room where two men he had recruited were waiting.

He laid Judith, half-conscious, on the bed and stripped off her clothes. The men, now naked, moved in while Naso sat in a chair, masturbating, his camera ready.

But when one held her down and the other mounted her, Judith fought back. Even drugged, she kicked and shoved, yelling until the men panicked and fled.

Still masturbating, Naso tried to convince her she had imagined it—that she had only been with him. But she'd seen him, standing there with his pants open, camera in hand. She knew.

When Naso told me this story, he laughed. "I don't think she believed me. She looked right at me while I stood there jacking off."

I asked him directly, "So what was the plan? What did you want to prove? You drugged her—anything that happened wasn't her choice. You understand that, right?"

He dismissed me. "They're all whores. It just takes the right situation to bring it out."

But I saw something he wouldn't admit. Relief. Relief that Judith had resisted. Because if she hadn't—if she had shown the smallest sign of arousal, or if he'd convinced himself she enjoyed it—I believe he would have killed her, mother of his sons or not.

23

Sharieea: The Knock

Most murder victims know their killers. Husbands. Wives. Lovers. Friends. Murder, after all, is an intimate act, born of rage, jealousy, or betrayal. That's why detectives always start close to home. And most of the time, they're right. Ordinary killers aren't experts. They leave a trail of sloppy mistakes—fingerprints, blood, fibers—that lead straight to their door.

Serial killers are different. Their victims are strangers, chosen at random—or chosen for reasons no one else can understand. The triggers are buried deep in fantasy and obsession, a twisted mix of sex, power, and hate. You can profile them, but it won't stop them. Arrests don't come from psychology. They come from luck, from an eyewitness—or from science finally catching up to the evidence the killers left behind.

Investigators began breaking through cold cases not with a profiler's hunch but with DNA. Years of silence could be shattered by a single strand of genetic code.

Men like Joseph Naso kill for decades with almost no resistance. They move through the world unnoticed, ordinary on the surface, while carrying murder in their eyes.

In 1980, Naso moved to San Francisco. Divorced now, he was living rent-free as the manager of an apartment complex at 839 Leavenworth Street. The job required almost nothing of him, yet it placed him in the middle of a revolving door of tenants, transients, and strangers—an endless supply of potential victims, all just steps from his front door.

DATE: 1980–1981
LOCATION: San Francisco, California
NASO'S LIST: #7. Lady from 839 Leavenworth
VICTIM: Sharieea Patton
Part One: The Knock

For Naso, managing the complex was a "sweet gig." Not just for the free rent, but for the set of master keys—and the chance to feed his oldest obsession: stealing women's underwear. Now he could indulge whenever he wanted.

Within two weeks, he had memorized the tenants' routines—who left for work early, who stayed out late, who vanished on weekends. When the coast was clear, he slipped inside, always with a ready excuse about checking a fuse box or water main if someone happened to question him.

Once in, he took what he craved most. Small bills. Jewelry unlikely to be missed. But always underwear. Sometimes he lingered, stripping off his clothes, slipping into the women's lingerie, even crawling into their beds. In the space they thought was safe, he pleasured himself and left behind only the faintest trace of violation.

When tenants first met him, Joe put on the act he had perfected for years: a little odd, maybe eccentric, but harmless. That illusion was his camouflage. What most saw as a bumbling, slightly creepy man was in fact a cold predator waiting for the right opportunity.

That opportunity came with a knock on his door.

He almost bumped into her in the hallway as he returned with groceries. "Hi, I'm the manager," he said, shifting the bag and extending his hand. "Can I help you with something?"

"I'm Sharieea," she said. "I'm here about the apartment. Is it still available?"

As always, Joe sized her up. Every woman he met was a potential conquest, and this one excited him. She reminded him of Judith—not in her looks, but in her mannerisms and perfume. An "older broad," as he put it. She was in her fifties, and he was forty-six, but with his balding head and worn frame, he looked older.

"Yes, it is," he said, nodding. "Give me a second to put these things down, and I'll get the key."

He unlocked his door and waved her inside. The place looked less like an apartment than a studio—cameras on tripods, lights, mannequins set up as if waiting for a shoot.

"Are you a photographer?" she asked.

"Yes," he said from the kitchen. "A professional photographer. Actually, an artist. The business part is what you see. I also teach at the Academy of Art in the city."

"Wow. Impressive."

Naso came toward her with a magazine, page marked. "What do you do, if you don't mind my asking?"

"Not much anymore. I'm retired, but I used to work for the LA Sheriff's Department."

That caught him off guard. "You a cop?"

She shook her head quickly. "No, just a clerk. I was living with my daughter near Lake Tahoe, but we had a falling out and I moved here. My pension's small, so I've been applying for jobs around town to get by."

His pulse eased—nothing to worry about. "From last year," he said, handing her the magazine. "My work's been in several magazines. I work constantly—that's why you see all this." He gestured toward the setup. "You could say I bring my work home with me." He extended his hand again. "By the way, I'm Joe. Please call me Joe."

"Pleasure to meet you, Joe the artist," she said, shaking his hand.

He gave her a practiced smile. "Let me show you the apartment."

Sharieea walked through the unit, considering the space. Naso wasn't interested in her opinion—he was studying the sway of her body, the jiggle of her breasts. From the start, he had made up his mind to have sex with her. If she agreed, good. If not, he would take what he wanted. Simple.

She signed the lease and paid first and last month's rent, plus a security deposit.

When she moved in a week later, Naso handed her an envelope. "It's the security deposit," he whispered with a wink. "Sometimes a small gesture of kindness is all we need to make our day. I hope it helps."

She hugged him in gratitude, even kissed him. He hugged her back, savoring the feel of her body against his.

Within two weeks of moving in, she asked Joe to replace a faulty light switch. Unlike most tenant requests, this one got his attention. He was at her door immediately.

She offered him coffee, and while he worked, she mentioned her pension wasn't enough to cover expenses. Bills were piling up, and she still hadn't found steady work. She was afraid she'd have to find a cheaper place.

Joe listened, studying her body as much as her words. He'd dealt with women who needed money before. Desperation always opened the same door. In his mind, women exaggerated their problems just to lure a man into rescuing them. He figured she was doing the same.

He'd also noticed her late nights, the way she went out dressed up and came back hours later. To him, that meant only one thing: she was hustling on the side. Whether it was true or not didn't matter. He believed it, and that belief was enough.

One afternoon, when the subject of money came up again, he made his play.

"You know," he said, leaning back in his chair, "you could model for me. I pay my models a standard fee—fifty dollars for a ninety-minute session. A few sessions could go a long way."

She laughed. "I'm not a model, Joe."

He kept his expression serious. "I'm the artist, and you, my dear, are beautiful. Think it over—it could be fun."

She smiled, half teasing. "What, are you just trying to get me out of my clothes?"

Her coy reaction threw him. He shook his head quickly, keeping his tone calm, professional. "Of course not. I'm legit. I respect you and my work. You'd have nothing to worry about."

That seemed to settle it. "Okay, Joe. Let's give it a try. When do we start?"

"Tomorrow evening," he said at once. "Six o'clock. Bring three outfits—one evening dress."

Joe could barely contain his excitement. As soon as he left her apartment, he went straight to his own, pulled on a pair of her panties and a bra, and masturbated. He had taken them on one of his break-ins—slipping into her unit when she was gone, rummaging through her drawers, and helping himself. More than once, he had undressed in her bedroom, put on her underwear, and finished in her bed.

In his mind, wearing her clothes made him part of her, and her part of him.

The first session went smoothly. He followed the usual protocols—lighting, direction, nothing suggestive—just enough to keep her comfortable. But his mind was already plotting the next step: not just pictures, but her body, traded for a place to live.

Over the next few weeks, they met several times. Each shoot, he pushed a little further. During one of them, he complimented her body and she hugged him. When he tried to kiss her, she allowed it for a moment, but as his hand slid inside her dress, she pulled back.

"Please stop," she said firmly. "That's not what I want, Joe."

He forced a polite smile. "Of course. I'm sorry. You're beautiful—I lost my head. I don't want you to feel uncomfortable." He offered her the choice to leave, acting contrite, but inside he was boiling.

She hesitated. "It's getting late. Let's do this another night."

After she left, he posed a mannequin where she had stood and acted out the rest of the session as he wanted it: thrusting himself against it while wearing her stolen underwear, his hands wrapped around its throat. "Fuckin' whore, fuckin' bitch, now you'll die." He shook the mannequin violently until he climaxed.

Later, sipping coffee, he made up his mind. She had to die. She knew who he was, where he lived. If she went to the police, he was finished. Consent wasn't going to happen, so the only way forward was force.

But first, he wanted more pictures.

A couple of days later, Naso ran into her outside the laundry room.

"Hi, Joe," she said. "Got time for more pictures? I could use the work."

He tilted his head, making a show of considering it. "Maybe. I'll have to check my schedule." He was baiting the trap—the rent was coming due, and desperation would work in his favor.

She sighed. "It's been tough. After the holidays, no one's hiring."

He nodded, feigning sympathy. "Well, let me move some things around. If I can clear a slot, I'll give you a couple of hours."

She reached out and hugged him, thanking him.

For the next several days, he let her stew, saying nothing, only watching her frustration grow. In his mind, if she grew desperate enough, she would finally confirm what he already believed about all women—that at the core they were whores, ready to sell themselves when the need was sharp enough. And that would only make his decision easier.

A few evenings later, the knock came.

He opened his door, and there she was.

"Hi, Joe. Sorry to bother you, but you said you'd see if you could fit me in for another session. It's been almost a week."

The hook was set. "I'm sorry, it's been busy," he said. "It slipped my mind."

Her face fell. He let the silence hang and then added, "But if you're free tonight, maybe I can give you an hour of work."

"I appreciate that, Joe, but I need more than an hour. My rent's due, and I'm behind."

"How behind?"

"A hundred seventy-five dollars."

He studied her. Maybe she was hustling him, maybe not. Either way, she had come to him. That was all that mattered.

"That's a lot of money," he said carefully. "But maybe I can help. Come by tonight. We'll work something out."

She hugged him again, thanking him. He hugged her back, tasting the certainty of it—he would take her first. And then he would kill her.

24

Sharieea: The Coat

DATE January 1981
LOCATION: San Francisco, California
NASO'S LIST: #7. Lady from 839 Leavenworth
VICTIM: Sharieea Patton
Part Two: The Coat

That evening, Sharieea knocked on his door again. In her mind, it was about rent money. To him, it was about control.

He opened the door wearing a short-sleeved button-down and a turquoise choker strung with shells, the kind of thing a teenager might wear, not a balding middle-aged man. He didn't care.

"Hello, Sharieea," he said. "You look stunning."

She stepped inside, remarking on the cold. He took her coat and rubbed the rabbit fur against his cheek. "I love the feel—it's my favorite. Let's get started, my dear. And I've got some ideas to help with your financial situation."

He offered her a deal: two hundred dollars for a ninety-minute lingerie session. Then he handed her two new outfits, still boxed, and a portfolio of his work. "My photos are meant to highlight a woman's beauty—her true power."

She hesitated. "I'm nervous, Joe. "I've never posed in lingerie before." But she thumbed through the samples anyway.

"See?" he said. "Classy, nothing pornographic. And you're much more beautiful than any of these women." He reached for her hand. "Tell you what, I'll throw in another fifty."

That did it for her. She went to the bathroom to change.

By the time she came out, the living room was a full studio: lights, tripods, camera ready. He began shooting as she posed. The shutter clicked, and with every frame, he imagined the session leading where he wanted. Her poses grew more suggestive. She even blew him a kiss for the camera. In his mind, that meant she'd given him permission.

When he set the camera down and crossed to her, she let him take her hand. He guided her toward the armrest of the couch, and she smiled up at him. Then he bent to kiss her.

She pushed lightly at his chest. "Joe, please. I'm not interested in a relationship."

Naso smiled thinly. "Yes, of course. But I'm in control here, not you." He was done playing the role of a sucker.

She frowned at his words. The next moment, his hands were at her throat. He threw her back onto the couch, his weight pinning her down, his grip tightening. Her kicks were nothing. He squeezed until she blacked out.

"Fucking whore," he said, unbuckling his pants. "This is what you want."

He raped her while she was still unconscious. When she stirred and tried to fight, he cut off her scream with both hands at her throat. This time, he didn't stop until she was dead. To him, that was perfection.

He thrust into her again and again until he finally finished. As he stood over her, he caught his reflection in the full-length mirror on the wall.

"She got the Naso gold-standard fuck," he told himself. Doubling over, he laughed uncontrollably, barely able to stand.

Once he steadied himself, he moved on with his ritual. He stripped off his clothes, put on her stockings and panties, and took photographs of her body posed the way he wanted. Then came the coffee. With a cup in hand, he sat beside her and let the quiet take hold.

After a hot shower, he got dressed and began what he called "filing things under T—for trash." He stuffed all her clothes and personal items into a bag, keeping only a few, like her rabbit-fur coat. Next, he used stockings and plastic ties to bind her body into a fetal position and sealed it in trash bags.

It was just before 2 a.m. No one was around. Joe hauled everything to his car and drove toward Tiburon, near the bay shoreline. On the way, he slid in the *Riders on the Storm* cassette and sang along with Morrison.

He dumped her at the water's edge and drove off, pulling into a nearby McDonald's to toss her things into the dumpster. His last stop was a twenty-four-hour liquor store, where he bought coffee and powdered donuts. Back in his kitchen, he ate them, laughing while the sugar dusted the table.

"Killing whores is hard work," he muttered, giggling again.

"How did you get away with it?" I asked Naso. "Everyone knew you'd been with Sharieea. And everyone knew you photographed her. Yet you walked free."

He laughed. "Cops have shit for brains. Unless they get lucky, or stumble blindly into something important, you don't get caught."

"Yes, but they came to your place and questioned you about her. You had to know they'd come. Wasn't that a risk?"

"Not really," he said with a shrug. "Of course, I knew they'd show up. But by then, I'd dumped everything and hid the film and pictures. And the ones who came by? A couple of retards. I ran circles around them."

I leaned in. "Still, why take the chance? With Sharieea, the connection was obvious. She lived in your building. Everyone knew you managed the place. She posed for you in your apartment. That's not like the others. Why her?"

His eyes narrowed. "She got under my skin. I couldn't stop thinking about her. But the whore didn't want to let me fuck her. So I gave her what she really wanted." His voice rose, raw and biting. "She was faking—taking her clothes off for money, always wanting more to spread her legs. So I cut to the chase."

His words hung there, jagged with rage. I'd heard it before—in thousands of hours of conversation with him, whenever we touched the subject of rape or murder. The anger was always there, coiled just under the surface. Sometimes it came out as a sneer, sometimes a hiss. Here it tore through, unmasked.

And it was always sharper with her. Whenever I brought up the "Lady from 839 Leavenworth"—number seven on his handwritten list of ten—Naso grew agitated. Sharieea Patton had gotten under his skin in a way the others never did.

25

Sara

The day was gray and damp, the kind that made the concrete yard smell of mildew and rust. I was pushing Joe's wheelchair along the fence line, away from the card tables and the noise. He liked to talk where no one else could hear, twisting around in his seat to look up at me as I steered him along.

Joe was talking about rest periods again. Cops believed he stopped after Sharieea Patton in 1981 and didn't kill again until the nineties. He mocked that theory.

"They think they know when I stopped and when I started up again," he muttered. "Cops don't know shit. They're still going by that silly list."

He gave a sly grin. "But I never finished it."

I slowed my pace. "You didn't finish?" That was new. He'd never mentioned that before.

"Of course not. I lost the sheet of paper before I wrote the rest down."

The best way to keep him talking was to reaffirm that the cops had gotten it wrong. "That's incredible. Over a hundred investigators on your case, and not one of them realized the list might be incomplete—or not even the real body count."

"Not by a long shot. Idiots. I killed in the sixties, seventies, eighties, and nineties. Killer of the decades. Better than the Oakland Raiders, the team of the decades."

He looked smug, as if he'd just scored a point the cops would never get back. "That's what amazes me," he said. "They nail you for a murder, or a few, and they think that's it. Like that's all you've done. You'd have to be pretty damn stupid to get caught after only one."

I played to his ego. "Well, Joe, you didn't get caught after your first. Or your tenth. Or even your last."

He smirked. "Who said I was done?"

"Okay, you got me there. I just assumed you'd stopped—that you'd retired."

"Artists don't retire. We evolve. We find new ways to accomplish our goals."

As often happened, we'd veered off topic. The trick was to get him back on track without making him feel I was interrogating him. Sometimes it was better to change the subject and give him a break. I asked him if he wanted a cup of coffee and a peanut butter and Nutella sandwich I'd made.

"Oh, yes. You always have something good to eat."

While I got the hot water ready, I parked his wheelchair at the back of the yard, tucked into a corner to keep him isolated. Out of the corner of my eye, I saw him rise. There he went again, waltzing with his invisible partner, arms wrapped around empty air as he turned slow circles on the concrete. I let him finish before I came back over.

"Here you go, Joe. Taster's Choice and one of my special artist sandwiches." I handed both to him. "Enjoy that, and I'll help Mr. Carpenter get to medical."

He took the coffee, scowling. "Fuck Carpenter. Sit down and let's talk. What's he got that I don't?"

"Nothing," I said evenly. "He just needs help. But okay—fuck him. What's on your mind?"

Once he knew I wasn't leaving, he dug in. He ate the sandwich, sipped his coffee, and finally looked up. "That was wonderful, Bill," he said softly, his smile wet and toothless.

"Glad it hit the spot."

To my surprise, he jumped back on topic. "Back to rest periods. I didn't rest until '99. Just because the cops didn't find any of my girls doesn't mean I stopped. Blind luck—that's how they got Sara. Otherwise, they'd think I didn't kill again until '93.

I nodded. "Makes sense, but why not dump her where they'd find her, like some of the others? Why not show your work?"

He shrugged. "I didn't feel like it. Besides, I had their pictures. And it was easier to just leave them somewhere where they'd be forgotten. Most of them were just trash. Not worth remembering."

It struck me as not entirely true. There was something about those girls he hid from discovery that he wouldn't reveal to me. At least, not yet.

DATE: April 25, 1992
LOCATION: Interstate 80 outside Oakland, California
NASO'S LIST: #8. The Girl in Woodland (Near Nevada County)
VICTIM: Sara Dylan

Sara Dylan was on her way to a Bob Dylan concert in Seattle on April 27, 1992. She'd just seen him play Maui on the twenty-second and Waikiki on the twenty-fourth, then flown into Oakland. Friends later said she wanted to hitchhike the rest of the way north for the beginning of Dylan's West Coast Tour.

When I first heard what she'd planned, it didn't add up. Why stop in Oakland when Seattle was the goal? Why not fly straight through? And if she had money for planes and concerts, why stick out her thumb on I-80 with only two days to get there? That part always nagged at me. Maybe the ticking clock made her careless. Maybe that's why she climbed into the wrong car.

That afternoon Joseph Naso was returning home to Yuba City, driving northeast on I-80 after a day in Oakland. He'd shot two family sessions and stopped at a sports memorabilia show, filling his trunk with football and baseball collectibles from the 1950s and '60s.

On the way out of the Bay Area, he stopped off at a roadside fruit stand. Minutes later, as he steered back toward the interstate, he noticed her: a young woman in a sunhat, dress, and tennis shoes, holding a cardboard sign that read "Seattle, Washington."

Naso slowed and rolled down his window. "Seattle? That right?"

"Sure is," she said brightly, stepping closer to the car. "How far you going?"

He liked what he saw. "I can get you up to the 5, near Yuba City. That help?"

"It sure does."

"Hop in."

She swung open the door, dropped her backpack and sign to the floor, and slid in. "Thanks. I'm Sara," she said, offering her hand.

"Joe," he said, shaking it. "Headed all the way to Seattle?"

"Yeah. Meeting my friends at my brother's concert."

"Who's your brother?"

"Bob Dylan," she said without hesitation. She pulled out her license—"Sara Dylan"—and tapped the Bob Dylan pin on her dress. "I go to all his concerts."

Later, Naso told me, "I found out at the trial that she was lying, but at the time, she seemed like the real deal." Unlike other lies that gnawed at him, this one hadn't left him angry. He wanted to believe her, and the ID and pin gave him permission.

The thrill was what mattered. Naso loved brushing up against fame. He hoarded photos of himself with Wayne Newton, Michelle Pfeiffer, Glenn Close, Anthony Hopkins. He didn't know any of them, but the snapshots let him pretend he was part of their world. With "Bob Dylan's sister" in his passenger seat, the illusion was complete.

She talked easily as they merged back onto the interstate, describing her travels—France, Texas, Hawaii, Australia—always chasing the next concert. Naso stayed quiet, letting her talk, as his eyes drifted to her wrists, her hands, the way she moved in the seat.

He cranked the driver's-side window closed, sealing the car, wanting her scent to linger. Each word she spoke only stoked the pictures in his head—her beneath him, naked.

This was nothing new. Back in the 1950s he'd given rides to unsuspecting girls, taking what he wanted and moving on to the next. Yuba City had given him the same hunting ground all over again— only now it was highways instead of small-town roads. I-80. Highway 99. The long reach of I-5. Sometimes he went looking, and other times the prey appeared on its own. Like today.

When her eyes flicked to the camera gear piled in the back, he jumped at the chance to boast. "I'm a professional photographer," he said, straightening in the driver's seat. "Published in real magazines. Outdoor work's my specialty. Perfect light, perfect composition. Most people look right at the world and don't see a damn thing—until I show them."

Sara managed a polite nod. Maybe she believed him, maybe she didn't. But Joe grinned anyway, puffing his chest as he steered with one hand, pleased with himself.

As the miles slid by, she talked about her brother, about the music, about how she never stayed in one place for long. Joe listened, playing the kind, attentive old man. But in his head, the façade was already slipping. He wasn't thinking about her stories. He was deciding how to silence that cheerful voice.

Before long, they were nearing I-5, where he'd have to drop her off.

"Sara, you hungry? I know a place not far from here. My treat."

She paused and then said yes—good enough for him. He turned into a small fast-food restaurant. After ordering, they found a booth, and she carried the conversation while they ate. Joe watched her the whole time, quiet, patient, like a hawk studying a rabbit.

It was time to bait the trap. If she didn't take it, he always had plan B.

When she finished most of her meal, he leaned back with his coffee, his voice calm and casual. "Sara, it's getting a bit late. By the time we reach the 5, it'll be close to six and starting to get dark. No guarantee you'll catch a ride out there—and that's a bad place to be at night."

She tilted her head, weighing his words. "I'll be fine. I'll catch a ride before dark."

Joe gave a sympathetic nod. "Okay. But if you think you might get caught out there, I can offer you a room at my home for the night."

She forced a quick smile. "That's kind of you, but I need to keep moving." She pushed her tray aside and stood. "Mind if I hit the restroom before we go?"

"Of course," he said, hiding his disappointment. "Take your time. Want anything before we leave?"

"Sure, a large Pepsi. Thanks."

By the time Sara emerged, Joe was waiting at the entrance with the car idling. She climbed in, and he handed her the drink and pointed to a paper bag on the dash. "Got you some fries too," he said with a smile.

She brightened. "Thank you so much."

They returned to the highway, Sara sipping her drink, munching on the fries, and humming along to the tape she'd put into the cassette player. For a while she seemed relaxed, watching the sun sink low over the fields.

Then her words began to slow. The cup slipped a little in her hand. She blinked hard and shook her head, trying to focus on the road ahead.

Joe kept his eyes on the traffic, expression unchanged, the harmless old man still firmly in place. A low thrum of excitement rose in his chest. Plan B was working.

She shifted in her seat, murmured something he couldn't catch, and sagged against the window. Her eyelids fluttered. The song on the stereo played on, her voice trailing off mid-verse.

By the time Joe steered off onto a darker stretch of road, she was gone—slumped, breathing shallow, trapped in the fog he'd fed her. He pulled over, killed the engine, and leaned across the seat. Her head lolled as he tugged at her clothes and forced himself inside her.

She stirred, whispering a faint, slurred "No." Her voice sharpened suddenly, panic breaking through the fog. "Stop!" she cried, shoving at his chest.

"Fuckin' whore," he hissed.

Her nails raked his face, scratching at his eyes. "Get off me!" she screamed.

He smashed a fist across her cheek and clamped his hands around her throat. She kicked, clawed, fought, but he only squeezed harder.

Her hands fluttered weakly at him now, her body losing strength. The drug, the blow, the chokehold—together they dragged her down into silence. Her last ragged sounds tangled with the music still spilling from the stereo.

As life slipped from her body, Naso renewed his efforts, savoring the last moments. When she went still beneath him, he pulled back and zipped his pants. After catching his breath, he carried the large Pepsi cup outside and flung it into the weeds. No trace.

From the back seat he grabbed one of his small cameras, loaded film, and leaned over her body. He snapped shot after shot—her slack face, her bare skin, the stillness that excited him.

When he was finished, he heaved her limp weight into the trunk and climbed behind the wheel. For a moment he sat in the dark car, going through the contents of her pack. He pulled out her identification, studied the name—"Sara Dylan"—and slipped it into his pocket. The Bob Dylan pin followed, small but precious. His tokens.

Joe turned the key, and Dylan's voice filled the car again. With a quick jab, he hit "eject," sick of hearing it. He studied the label and then flicked the tape into the night—leaving behind a piece of the puzzle of what happened to Sara Dylan.

Hours later, on Highway 20, he veered off onto a narrow road that twisted into the Tahoe National Forest. The trees closed in, shadows swallowing the car. He cut the headlights and crept forward until he found a clearing.

He carried her into the brush, the moonlight bright enough to see every curve of her body, stirring him. He laid her down, stripped, and lowered himself onto her.

Afterward, he lay beside her in the dirt, staring at the stars, Dylan's song still running in his head. Without hurry, he dragged her to the edge of an embankment and shoved her over. She tumbled out of sight into the night.

More than a decade later, a jogger stumbled on a skull near Zeibright Road in the Tahoe National Forest. Another ten years passed before the truth of that April night finally caught up with Joseph Naso.

When I asked him about it, he said, "Yeah. I messed up. Shouldn't have kept the tokens."

He leaned closer, his crooked grin spreading. "I was lucky. If my storage locker hadn't been broken into, they'd have found all my memorabilia—every token. They'd have known it all." He laughed his high, grating giggle. "Damn, I miss my tokens. But I still got a few."

And just like that, he changed the subject. We were done talking about Sara Dylan.

26

Pamela: The Restaurant

How did Joseph Naso manage to elude authorities for so long?

He liked to say cops were stupid or lazy, but that was just his contempt for law enforcement talking. The truth was simpler—and darker. Most of the women he killed were prostitutes or addicts. The few who weren't had still agreed to pose for him, which, in his mind, made them no different. All of them were disposable.

And too often, law enforcement treated them the same way. Victims without stable families or safe reputations—sex workers, drug users, gang members—slipped down the priority list. "Play with fire, expect to get burned" was the mindset. When effort is rationed, those lives count for less.

Naso knew it. He exploited it. "They were whores," he told me flatly. "Trash that I took out. And the cops didn't give a shit either."

"But what about Sharieea Patton?" I asked him. "She wasn't a prostitute."

He shrugged. "Didn't matter. The cops thought she was, so they treated her like the rest."

"How can you be so sure?"

"They asked me if I'd paid her for sex and if she had a pimp."

Their bias gave him cover. Naso was her neighbor, their number-one suspect, a man with prior sexual assault charges who had photographed her repeatedly. Still, they did little to pursue her case.

It wasn't luck or cunning that kept him free. It was something worse: indifference.

That indifference swallowed Pamela Parsons too, her case left to gather dust for nearly twenty years before it was finally tied to Naso. She had a name and a life. But in Naso's ledger, she was reduced to a line: "the girl from Linda," number nine. He circled back to her story often, the details never shifting.

This is what he told me.

DATE: April 1993
LOCATION: Linda, California
NASO'S LIST: #9. The Girl from Linda (Yuba County)
VICTIM: Pamela Parsons
Part One: The Restaurant

It was a Saturday in mid-April 1993 when Naso first noticed her—a waitress he sized up as somewhere in her thirties, older than most of the girls he usually chased. He remembered the date clearly because he'd spent the afternoon at an Oakland A's game and later wandered into a small restaurant he knew well.

She came to his table, pen poised. "Ready to order?"

"Yes, honey," he said, his tone dripping with suggestion. "How about a large piece of cherry pie, a patty melt, and a vanilla shake."

"Would you like coffee with that?" she asked evenly, not giving him the reaction he wanted.

"Sure."

She scribbled quickly and turned away. Naso's eyes stayed fixed on her, lingering on the sway of her hips as she crossed the floor.

When she returned with his food, he leaned back from the plate. "What's your name, honey?"

She reached automatically for her chest, only then realizing she'd forgotten her name tag. "Pamela," she said, smiling.

"It's nice to meet you. I'm Joe."

She gave him a quick nod. "Enjoy your meal. Let me know if you need anything else."

He came back the next night. And the night after that. Over time, he observed her more closely, building a private case against her. To Naso, every kindness was a ploy, every smile a lie. When he learned she was also hustling for drugs and turning tricks to pay for them, it only confirmed what he already believed: women lived by deception.

But he didn't move on her quickly, not as he had with many of his victims. He wanted to taste the deception slowly, savor it like a game of cat and mouse.

"Why wait?" I asked him.

He met my eyes. "It made it sweeter to watch her work me, thinking she had the power. She had no idea who I was, or what I could do. When the time came, I'd even the score. I always do."

Still, he insisted Pamela as different. "She had a bit of good in her," he said. "She wasn't completely cold and corrupt. She was a whore, but she also worked a regular job bringing people their meals. I wanted to see if she would change."

"Hold up. You killed eighteen-year-old girls because you thought they were liars and whores and needed to be 'cleaned.' But Pamela was thirty-eight. She wasn't going to change, according to your own standards. What aren't you telling me?"

He dodged the question every time. But across years of conversations, a pattern emerged. Naso felt something for Pamela. One moment he fantasized about a normal relationship with her, and the next, he seethed with contempt. Back and forth he went, just as she did with drugs—using and then wanting to stop.

That conflict showed in how long he held off. After a couple of weeks of talking and flirting with her at the diner, he offered to pay for a modeling session. To that point, nothing had happened between them beyond ordering food and small talk.

It's impossible to know exactly what was going through the mind of a nearly sixty-year-old serial killer with more than twenty kills behind him. But whatever it was, it was enough to keep the monster beneath the surface—for a time.

On April 30, 1993, Naso drove to Pamela's home on North Beale Road in Linda, California, just minutes from where he lived. He was in a good mood, his imagination running ahead of him. In his mind, he wasn't an aging, balding man in his late fifties—he was young again, handsome, taking photographs of a thirty-something waitress who would soon fall for him. She'd praise his work, proclaim her love, and give herself to him.

When he arrived, he set up his camera gear and handed Pamela a small gift: a bottle of White Shoulders perfume, his favorite.

She smiled politely, but it wasn't what she wanted. The gift meant nothing to her. She was there for one reason—money.

For two hours he photographed her in lingerie, shifting outfits while she grew increasingly impatient. Pamela wasn't a teenager hoping the lens would transform her into a model—she was a woman waiting to be paid so she could feed the meth habit that was tightening its grip.

When the session ended, Naso lingered, hoping something more might happen. But she brushed him off, claiming she had to get to work, and asked him to leave.

He did—but only to his car. Moments later, he watched her drive off, park a short distance away, and make a quick exchange for drugs.

Over the months that followed, Naso returned again and again. He flirted, took more photographs, and stalked her from afar. Sometimes he caught her climbing into cars with men, and other times he watched her complete the transaction himself. For him, it was proof of the lies he always saw in women. For her, it was survival.

At the end of August 1993, Naso changed his tactics. The foolish fantasy he'd been nursing—of Pamela as something more than the others—dropped away. Now he decided to make her "perfect." But first, he wanted to experience her fully for who and what she was.

He tracked down the dealer he'd seen her buy from and asked for two grams of meth. At first the man shook his head, suspicious. "You a cop?"

Naso laughed and leaned in. "Nah. I just want to get a girl to suck my dick."

That answer did the trick. Fifty dollars later, the dope was his.

Armed with what he needed, Naso went to the restaurant. He slipped into his usual booth, the one where he could watch her work the floor. She came over with her pad ready.

"What'll it be, Joe?"

He lowered his voice. "Got something different for you, sweetheart." He reached into his jacket just far enough to let her glimpse the small plastic bag. The crystalline powder caught the light for an instant before he closed his hand.

Her eyes flicked to it, then back to him. "You serious?"

"Plenty more where this came from," he said. "We can have a little fun after your shift."

She hesitated only a second. "Pick me up at seven. Out back."

Naso grinned, the trap sprung. "I'll see you soon, Pamela."

On his way to the car, the thought of squeezing the life out of her overwhelmed him. He masturbated in the driver's seat, replaying the moment that was coming.

Just before seven, he pulled into the rear parking lot. Pamela slid into his car without a word, settling close. "Can I get a taste before we get to your place?" she asked, rubbing him through his pants.

He handed her a gram. She fished out a glass pipe, lit up, and inhaled deep.

At Naso's home, she got higher still. He poured drinks, and she downed them quickly, letting the alcohol blur the edges even more. Soon she was in his bed.

This time, Naso showed her a side she hadn't seen before—kinky, controlling. At one point he tied her hands with pantyhose.

Then she made the mistake.

"Choke me."

Those two words detonated something inside him. Rage. Validation. Hatred. They confirmed everything he believed about women. It was the trigger behind every rape, every assault, every murder.

He could have killed her then, but he held back. He wanted it to last. But in his mind, her fate was sealed. Soon, he would make her perfect.

27

Pamela: The Pose

DATE: September 15, 1993
LOCATION: Linda, California
NASO'S LIST: #9. The Girl from Linda (Yuba County)
VICTIM: Pamela Parsons
Part Two: The Pose

Over the next four weeks, Naso saw Pamela several times. But it wasn't until Wednesday, September 15, 1993, that his hatred fully emerged. He picked her up that afternoon and brought her to his home for what he described as "photos and fun." She knew the routine—lingerie, drugs, money, sex, and his camera.

The difference that night was simple: He had decided she would not leave alive. He wanted her final pictures to show her deception on full display.

He came out of the bathroom and caught her reflection in the mirror. She was bent over the pipe, inhaling smoke, her body showing the toll of years of use. He raised the camera and clicked a few frames and then unbuckled his pants. She didn't hesitate, moving to service him as she had before.

Watching her, he imagined her with all the other men. Fuckin' whore was a vampire. He had to clean her, erase the mess she'd become.

Holding back his climax, he put her on her hands and knees and looped the pantyhose around her neck. At first she took it as part of the game, the way she had before. But he didn't let go. He pulled tighter, thrusting harder, until her breath hitched and turned to gasps. She pawed at her throat, pitching forward in a panic to break free.

"No more games," he said, weighing her down, his grip cinching tighter. Grunting, she rolled to the side and for a moment he lost hold. She ripped off the pantyhose and dragged in air, scrambling to rise, to call out.

Naso smashed her head, pinned her flat, and wrapped his hands around her throat. This time he held on until the fight drained from her.

Even after she was gone, he didn't stop. He kept at her body, relentless. Finally, he turned to the routine that never changed: photographing, posing, talking as if the dead could answer. They always listened so well.

Over the next hour, he gathered her clothes, purse, and anything she'd touched, sealing it all in a plastic bag. Near two in the morning, he wrapped her in an old blanket, loaded her into the trunk, and started the drive toward the Yuba River.

On the way, he cued up *Riders on the Storm*, and Morrison's voice was with him once again. When Naso reached a spot he liked, he lingered in the car, reliving the kill. Only when he'd satisfied himself did he open the trunk, haul her out, and drag her into the brush—humming the song as he left her there and returned to his car.

Four days later, a man walking his dog discovered Pamela's naked body. Her arms were crossed over her chest.

When I asked Naso about that detail, he smirked and folded his own arms in demonstration. "She was a vampire. You should've seen her suck. Vampires sleep like that." He closed his eyes, posed like a corpse, and then opened one eye and burst out laughing.

28

Tracy

One day, I was cuffed behind my back on the first tier of East Block, heading to a medical appointment, when the alarms erupted. My escort told me to stand fast and then bolted outside. On the yard, gang members were stabbing each other, and the guards scrambled to stop the bloodshed. The gunner watched me from above, so I knew I'd be stuck for a while.

That's when I realized I was only a few steps from 1-EB-80—Naso's cell. I motioned to the gunner that I wanted to take a few steps closer. He gave the slightest nod, and I moved.

Here was my chance to see what Joe did when he thought no one was looking.

I moved closer, careful. But his neighbor "Bumpy," named for the bumps covering his face and body, spotted me. "Hey, Bill, what you doin' down here?"

Shit. Cover blown.

"Just cruising around," I muttered.

By then, Naso was already at the bars. "You're not supposed to be down here," he said.

"Yeah, I know. I'm escaping. Wanna come along?"

He chuckled. I was already peering past him into his cell. It was the same clutter I'd seen before, boxes piled like barricades, the putrid stink of sour milk and sweat hanging in the air.

But what caught me were the pictures.

All three walls were plastered with them. Photos of women, some posed, some crime-scene shots. And in the center of each collage, the same image of him from the 1970s, camera in hand, a red string stretched from his photo to theirs. The string made it seem as if he were still tethered to them, even in death, the connection unbroken.

Unlike most serial killers I'd known, who kept their obsessions hidden—or, like Ramirez and Bittaker, cloaked them in "celebrity"—Naso flaunted his in the open. If his behavior on the outside was anything like this, it's easy to see why his former neighbors called him "Crazy Joe."

I scanned the faces staring back at me.

Roxene Roggasch.

Sharieea Patton.

Pamela Parsons.

Carmen Colon.

Sara Dylan.

And many others.

I let the silence stretch.

"Nice work, Joe."

He turned to glance at them. "Just a few of my friends I like to keep around."

I motioned with my chin toward one of the photos near the bars. "Who's that?"

He chuckled to himself. "That's Tracy. What, I never told you about her? She wasn't all there."

"You mean she was crazy?"

"No, she was missing a finger. Get it? Not all there." He burst out laughing as if he'd just told the funniest joke in the world.

I stared at him, hate burning in my chest. The man really needed to die. No good would come from him remaining in this world.

A few days later, he came up to me in the yard with a handful of

Saw Naso's cell. He lives on
the first tier of East Block.
pictures of victims, women he
photographed and his art are all
taped to his walls.

His cell is a mess. His a
hoarder. Cardboard boxes line the
floor of his cell like carpet.
Says he doesn't like his feet to
touch the floor. However, he has
his trophies. They're on his walls.
He's always writing notes. Tapes them
next to pictures on walls. He's re-living
his crimes. — He has access to all

My journal: Naso's cell.

pictures. "Remember the girl who wasn't all there?" He burst out laughing again. "Let me tell you about her."

DATE: July–August 1994
LOCATION: Marysville, California
NASO'S LIST: #10. The Girl from MRSV (Cemetery)
VICTIM: Tracy Tafoya

On a July evening in 1994, Naso sat in his car in a Marysville supermarket lot, less than five miles from where he had dumped Pamela Parsons the year before. Now sixty, he was waiting for a buyer to take the Glock 10 and 9 mm stashed in his trunk—the same trunk that had carried Pamela's body.

The man was late, but Naso didn't mind waiting. Patience had carried him through years of hustling guns on the side—one of his fixations, right alongside women, sports memorabilia, and coins. He'd studied them, bought them, sold them, collected them. It had all started in 1953, when the Air Force put his first real weapon in his hands and he learned the kind of power a small piece of steel could hold.

Hot and restless, he finally stepped inside the market. The blast of air-conditioning brought him a rush of relief. He grabbed two wine coolers and moved toward the register, palming a candy bar and gum on the way.

Back in the heat, he nearly collided with a younger woman coming in.

"Oh, I'm sorry, honey, I didn't see you," he said.

"No worries, handsome." She smiled and walked on, her miniskirt catching his eye.

Decades of hunting had taught him how to spot a working girl. She fit the profile. Early thirties, he guessed. He was about to follow her when the gun collector pulled in. With a last glance at her legs, he turned back to business.

Once the deal was done, he prowled the streets searching for her. Not that night. But he knew she'd turn up.

Two days later, he spotted her outside the State Theatre, leaning against the wall, watching the traffic. He pulled to the curb, and she came right to his window.

"Hey, I know you," she said with a smile.

"Yes. I didn't get the chance to introduce myself the other day. I'm Joe—and I've been looking for you."

"You have? I'm Tracy. What's on your mind, handsome?"

"Oh, a little fun."

"Sounds great. I'm all about fun."

"Get in."

For the next couple of weeks, Naso saw her often. Sex, lingerie shots, poses he pushed further each time. His anger coiled tighter, and the games grew crueler: choking, bindings, control. When she wasn't in his bed, he was outside her house, watching from the street, peering through her windows in the dark.

"She was such a lying whore," he told me later. "I gave her the Naso touch." Then he snorted, pleased with himself.

By August, his anger toward her burned hot.

On Saturday, August 6, he caught sight of her on the main drag in Marysville, talking to a man on the sidewalk. Rage tightened his body. He honked, and the man glared. Tracy saw Joe, waved, and hurried over.

"Hey handsome, feel like a little fun tonight?" she asked, settling in beside him. She reached over and stroked him. "Wow, you're always so hard—saving it all for me?"

Naso smiled. But not for her. He knew he would kill her that night, and she'd be his forever.

At his place, he set out lingerie and gave her drugs to lower her guard. She posed, stripped, and wore the stockings he loved. Then he handed her a choker, and she slipped it on without hesitation.

That was all it took.

The rage inside him surged. He cast the camera aside and ripped at his shirt. Tracy stripped it from him, unbuckled his pants, and dragged them down. Each piece of clothing fueled his fury. She was stealing his control. When she pulled away his underwear, his hatred nearly consumed him.

They had sex—rough, urgent. Then he stopped cold and climbed off her.

"Joe, is everything okay?" she asked, startled.

It wasn't.

He snatched up a pair of stockings, tied her wrists and ankles, and shoved her onto her back. When he mounted her again, the choker was in his hands. He tightened his grip, her eyes widening as she kicked and fought for air.

He thrust harder and drove her into the headboard, spitting the words he always did. "Fuckin' whore, fuckin' bitch."

Her body spasmed around him—the death shakes. For him, it was the perfect release. For Tracy, it was the end.

Once he was sure she was dead, he glanced at his watch. 11:25. Plenty of time.

He made his usual cup of coffee and sat with her. Then he picked up his camera and photographed her, posing her to fit his fantasies. Through his lens, she was perfect.

Marysville Cemetery—that's where he would leave her.

Later he told me why: It reminded him of the first girl he'd raped decades earlier. "I wanted to be able to come back and pay my respects," he said, laughing, pumping his hand in a crude gesture. "Get it? Pay my respects?"

I could barely stand to listen. And yet the worst was still to come.

After his ritual shower, Naso gathered Tracy's belongings in a plastic bag. At 2:16 a.m., he laid her on the passenger-side floor and drove six miles to the cemetery off Highway 70. He had dreamed of this night. Now it was here.

Under a new moon—the kind of darkness that made him feel invisible—he lifted her onto the seat beside him and uncovered her. He paused to admire his work, then lowered his pants and had sex with the corpse, blind to the risk of discovery.

Suddenly headlights swept the lot. Joe scrambled into the driver's seat and sped off.

But the compulsion dragged him back.

Near the cemetery entrance, he stopped again. Propping Tracy upright against the passenger door, he pressed down hard on the gas. At the right moment, he shoved her out into the dark. In his mirror, he watched her body tumble, rolling into a drainage ditch where it came to rest.

"Why did you push her out of the car?" I asked Naso.

He smirked. "I saw a cartoon once of a body being pushed out of a car and it bounced. I wanted to see if that would really happen."

Tracy's body lay where he left her for nearly a week. On the morning of August 14, 1994, she was found naked, face down, decomposing in the summer heat. Animals and insects had torn at her. By the time she reached the coroner's office, no evidence could tie her death to Joseph Naso. He tossed his usual caution aside and still got away with it—at least for the moment.

29

Rachel

Rarely does a serial killer retire before he's caught. Time is the one adversary they can't outwit. As they age, their bodies weaken, their reflexes slow, and even their hunger for risk begins to dull.

Some criminologists believe that's why the Golden State Killer stopped. In the 1970s he terrorized California—raping, murdering, even taking on men as well as women. In the mid-1980s, his trail went cold.

Investigators suspected he may have grown too old to overpower his victims, or that he'd become wary of the new forensic science beginning to ensnare other killers. For forty years he lived undetected until a genealogy site linked DNA to him—a former cop hiding in plain sight.

Joseph Naso's path traced the same decline. According to him, his last kill came in 1999. By then, he was sixty-five, living in Sacramento. He'd moved there two years earlier under probation, forced to keep reporting for the compulsion he could never control: stealing.

That fall, the old man drove east on I-80 into the Sierra Nevada, pulled off near Donner Pass Road, and, in the thin mountain air, the years caught up to him, his edge all but gone.

⸺⁂⸺

William A. Noguera

Joseph Naso's 1999 California driver's license.

DATE: September 1999
LOCATION: Sierra Nevada, California
NASO'S LIST: Not included
VICTIM: Rachel

Naso climbed into his pickup for a run to Nevada, hoping to buy an 1860 Colt revolver for his collection and sell two others. The 9 mm he carried stayed with him always—insurance after a close call the year before, when two young men robbed him and took his guns. He hadn't reported it. A parolee with firearms risked prison, and the scrutiny would have exposed years of buying and selling weapons. Carrying the pistol was a gamble, but one he was willing to take.

Just outside Sacramento, he saw her. A woman in her mid-twenties, thumb out on the side of the highway. Tall, confident, striking, and wearing an Air Force jacket heavy with stripes and chevrons.

He pulled over. For most veterans, the uniform meant service, camaraderie, maybe combat. For Naso, it meant something darker: rapes and assault. When she leaned toward his window, the jacket brought it all back.

"Where you headed?" he asked with a smile.

"Reno," she said, brushing her fingers through her hair. "How far can you take me?"

The gesture made his pulse quicken. She had no idea the danger she was in, and he loved it.

"I'm going that way," Naso said. "Jump in."

She slid into the passenger seat, her eyes drifting to the camera on the dash and the leather case on the floor. "I'm Rachel," she said warmly. "Looks like you're a photographer?"

He nodded smoothly, the practiced smile quick to his face. "Joe. Yes—a professional photographer."

"Really? What kind do you do?"

He put his arm over the back of the seat, leaning just close enough to test her comfort, and slipped easily into the story. "Family portraits in the beginning," he said, moving into the lies: years as the Oakland A's photographer, fashion shoots for Ford, even a gallery show in New York. The words rolled off his tongue, polished by repetition. He watched her face as he spoke, feeding on her little smiles and nods.

"Wow, impressive," she said. "Are you heading to a shoot now?"

"No," he said. "Just a road trip—capturing the beauty of California before the century ends. A personal project I'll be showing at an exhibit in New York next month."

Her eyes lit up. "Awesome. I'd love to see your work someday."

Naso was baiting the trap, but his focus kept slipping. All he could think about was this girl's body beneath him. He forced a smile. "Tell me about yourself. I see the Air Force uniform. Did you serve?"

"A couple years back," she said with a shrug. "But I just like my old uniform. So I added a few things to make it fashionable."

He didn't know why, but he knew she was lying. "So you were a staff sergeant, huh? Did you like the Air Force?"

"Yeah, it was fine, but it's not who I am anymore. Too much of what I saw overseas—it changes how you look at people." Her expression clouded, then she pushed it away.

"Did you serve long? Staff sergeant takes some time to earn."

"Six years. But that's all behind me now." She changed the subject quickly. "Are you going to stop and get shots of the redwoods and pines? I love how small they make you feel."

Inside, Naso's doubts hardened. Six years didn't fit—she would've reenlisted or explained why she hadn't. And twice now he'd called her a staff sergeant when she clearly wore master sergeant stripes. No one who'd earned that rank would've let it slide. She hadn't corrected him once.

She might have served, but that jacket? Probably thrift-store surplus. A borrowed honor draped across a liar's shoulders. His stomach twisted with hate.

They stopped to pick up food and beer. When she shrugged off the jacket, his eyes ran over her body, measuring her strength as much as her curves. She was strong, and the threat of it gnawed at him. She didn't have to do anything—her very presence pushed him off balance, taking his control. He despised her for it.

A little past the halfway mark, Naso decided to test her and see how she responded. He spotted a stretch of trees—the perfect place for a trial run of his plan.

"This is a beautiful area," he said lightly. "Would you mind if I stopped for a few shots?"

"No, not at all."

At the next exit he turned off, followed a well-kept dirt road into the forest, and stopped in a grove of evergreens. Grabbing his camera and a couple of lenses, he climbed out.

"This is just beautiful," he said, glancing around. "See? Even at the end of the twentieth century, you can still find a little slice of heaven right here on Earth."

"It really is," Rachel said, stretching as she got out.

A few yards away, he framed the trees and sky, and then swung the lens toward her. She noticed and smiled, even posing against a tree. When he handed her the camera, she scrolled through the shots, laughing at herself, pleased with what she saw.

Soon they were back on the highway, the radio filling the cab, mile after mile, until she turned it up for a song she loved. She sang along, tapping her fingers against the door, her voice light and unguarded. For her, it was a moment of freedom on the open road.

The lyrics slammed into him. "Clean again." His grip on the wheel tightened, his knuckles pale. This confirmed it. In his mind, the decision was already made. He would make her perfect.

Nearing Donner Lake, he turned off onto a fire road. The Tahoe National Forest stretched around them, the sun sinking fast, threatening to vanish behind the high peaks. A chill carried the edge of autumn as he pulled into a clearing.

Rachel opened the passenger door and started to get out, but Naso stopped her.

"Here," he said, handing her the camera. "Take a look—you'll see it differently through the lens."

"Oh, cool," she said, slipping it into her hands. "Thanks."

She walked a short distance and lifted it to her face, peering through the lens at the wooded landscape.

Naso reached behind the seat, drew out the 9 mm from its hiding place, and slid it into his camera case. A flicker of unease edged in— she wasn't like the others, not prey he could control without doubt. The pistol was his compensation, the crutch of an aging killer who still heard the call and couldn't resist answering it.

He came up to her just as she focused the camera on him and clicked the shutter. "Don't shoot!" he joked, raising both hands. "I'm unarmed."

She laughed, lowering the camera. For a moment they looked like two friends enjoying themselves. She couldn't have known that the man smiling back at her was intent on rape and murder.

They came to a fallen Jeffrey pine with its roots exposed and tangled across another giant trunk, forming a rough wooden cross. Joe snapped closeups of the trees, then aimed the lens at her. He stepped in for a close shot of her face and, taking advantage of the nearness, leaned in to kiss her.

She shoved him hard. "Hey, what are you doing, you perv?"

The force of it staggered him backward over a root, making him drop his camera. Rage surged hot and humiliating. She wasn't just pushing him away—she was exposing him. Pretender, fraud, old man with nothing left.

He hauled himself up, fists clenched, and lunged. But she was faster. Her kick drove into his gut, folding him in half.

"Fuckin' pervert piece of shit," she said, turning away from him, her voice loud and scornful. "Don't touch me or I'll beat your old ass."

He yanked the 9 mm from the case and followed. Another lying whore daring to act like she was better than him.

She spun to face him, steady in her stance. Clearly trained. But Naso smiled. Still no match for a bullet.

He raised the gun. "Take off the jacket," he growled.

"Fuck you. I'm not doing shit, you asshole."

Her defiance stopped him cold. For a second, he just stared, dumbfounded. Every other woman he'd controlled had broken, shown fear. This one hadn't. She gave him only contempt.

The shock curdled into rage. He swung the pistol and struck her, opening a gash at her temple.

"I said take off the jacket!" he shouted.

This time she slowly complied, blood trickling down her cheek, but her eyes still held nothing but disgust. No fear. And he hated her for it.

"Take off the rest."

When she just stared, he grabbed her by the throat and pressed the gun to her face.

Her eyes never blinked. "Fuck you, perv." She spat on his face.

He hit her again. She crumpled. He tore at her clothes and threw himself on top of her, but his body betrayed him. No erection. No power. The mask of the predator cracked wide open, leaving only an old man scrambling in humiliation.

She came to and bucked him off, her kick catching him in the face and throwing him back. "Get off me, you fuckin' cocksucker!" she yelled.

Pain flashed white. He lurched up, furious, reaching for the pistol.

Three shots shattered the forest silence. Rachel collapsed, chest torn open.

"Fuckin' whore," he hissed. "Thought you could fool me. Pretend to be a soldier, act like you're better than me. You ruined it. You fuckin' ruined it."

When the rage ebbed, he steadied his breathing, collected the camera, and slid the pistol back into its case. He stood over Rachel. "What a waste." He dragged her by the wrist into the brush, hidden beneath pines, then took her jacket and purse. The $140 in cash and her ID went into his pocket. The rest he dumped in Reno, behind a McDonald's, where he used her money to buy dinner.

I tried more than once to talk again about Rachel, but Naso shut me down every time. It was clear he regretted telling me. Once the story was out, though, he couldn't pull it back.

For years, his murders had ended the same way—posing the bodies, photographing them, capturing his triumph. But not this time. Rachel had fought too hard, left him too shaken. There were no photos. No ritual. Just rage, bullets, and silence in the trees.

Early on, I'd asked Joe why he choked his victims instead of stabbing or shooting them. He got animated, describing strangulation as the most natural act. "I can pin them down and drive my weight into them while I choke. You can feel it when they're going—the body grabs tight, contracts around you. It's too messy to stab or shoot. I'm silent when I work. I'm a professional."

That was how he saw himself: an executive whose "office" was wherever he stalked, raped, and killed. By shooting Rachel, he shattered his own code. She had broken him in a way no one else ever had.

My journal: choking versus stabbing or shooting.

30

The Arrest

After killing Rachel in 1999, Naso got spooked. Everything about her had gone wrong, and the insecurities he had smothered for years rose up to choke him. Each time he picked up a girl for sex, his body failed him. To Naso, it wasn't just impotence. At sixty-five, he could no longer deny that women found him repulsive.

Rachel's resistance had done what decades of investigations had not—it ended his reign of terror.

For the next decade, he drifted, moving twice within California before petitioning to relocate to Reno, Nevada. On paper, he wasn't a threat. His only convictions were for petty theft, usually women's underwear. He told clerks he "needed them for his girls." Authorities approved the move.

But the urge never stopped. Within days in Reno, he was caught pocketing small items from a store, even though he had cash in his pocket. The responding officer described him as "creepy and dirty" but let him go when a record check came back clean. No one imagined this frail shoplifter had murdered twenty-six women.

The irony was brutal. For fifty years he raped and killed without being caught. Petty theft—his other obsession—was his undoing.

When I confronted Naso about stealing, he denied it flatly—even when I told him I'd watched him pocket stamps and peanut butter packs from other inmates. His voice rose with anger, as if I'd accused him of something beneath him. To me, that reaction said everything. In private, he had admitted to me that he was a rapist and a killer, yet he couldn't bring himself to own up to petty theft. It was proof of how uncontrollable the compulsion was—an itch he couldn't stop scratching, and one he was ashamed to admit he couldn't control.

By 2009, Naso was living at 350 Medgar Avenue in Reno, a run-down house that reflected his filth and hoarding. Piles of junk, filthy clothes, and broken furniture made the place nearly unlivable. Anyone who has seen his cell on death row would recognize it instantly—the same squalor, only magnified. His son Charles, who suffered from schizophrenia, sometimes stayed there, though not full-time as Naso liked to claim. Because of repeated offenses, his probation officer, Wes Jackson, began making unannounced visits.

He returned in December 2009 and inspected the home but found nothing out of the ordinary—nothing that seemed to connect Naso to any serious crime.

After four months with no contact, Jackson appeared at the front door again on April 13, 2010, for another inspection. This time Naso looked rattled but let him in. A quick search of the living room turned up a single round of .380 ammunition—a clear violation. Jackson could have arrested him on the spot, but something made him pause. He studied the bullet, turning it in his hand. His instincts told him there was more here than an old shoplifter breaking the rules. He called for backup.

When the other officers from the Department of Parole and Probation arrived, they kept digging. Another round of ammunition surfaced, which Naso tried to pass off as belonging to his son Charles. But the second round's location set off alarms in Jackson's head. If there were more bullets, there might be a gun. He searched Naso himself, fearing the old man might be armed. No gun turned up, but in Naso's shirt pocket he found a slip of paper: a classified ad for a firearm.

Faced with the evidence, Naso rejected it all, claiming ignorance. He insisted he hadn't known he couldn't possess ammunition, and since he didn't have a gun, the bullets were harmless. That argument collapsed

Naso's Reno home: 350 Medgar Avenue.

when Jackson dialed the number on the ad. The seller picked up and confirmed that Naso had indeed tried to buy the weapon.

Jackson had seen enough. He snapped handcuffs on Naso's wrists and booked him for multiple probation violations that would keep him in jail for the next year. While he was being processed at the Washoe County jail, he continued to profess his innocence. The bullets were harmless, the gun ad meaningless, the officers mistaken. To him, it was all a misunderstanding.

What he didn't know was that even as he denied everything, investigators were still tearing apart his Reno home.

They soon discovered the real horror.

First came the photographs—thousands of them—women in lingerie, women bound, some appearing lifeless. The deeper they searched, the stranger it became. Mannequins were posed and tied as if they were captives, echoing the scenes in the photographs. In a binder, investigators found newspaper clippings about murdered women, carefully cut and preserved.

In the bedroom, they uncovered what would come to be known as *Naso's Rape Journal*—a handwritten chronicle of assaults stretching back to the 1950s. The search also turned up an arsenal: in his barn, behind a refrigerator and inside a wall, four guns were hidden. Throughout the house, they found knives and other weapons.

Two metal boxes yielded more than $150,000 in cash and a coin collection valued at around $30,000. But the most chilling discovery was a single sheet of lined paper in Naso's handwriting—a list of ten women, or, as he told me, "nine girls and one lady."

A multi-agency task force was formed—FBI, Washoe County in Nevada, and Contra Costa, Marin, and Yuba counties in California—all pouring resources into the case. While Naso sat in his cell convinced he was locked up on a routine probation bust, investigators worked furiously to connect the evidence before his release could threaten to close it all down.

Search warrants opened his safe deposit boxes, yielding women's IDs, passports, purses, newspaper clippings, and a Bob Dylan pin tucked beside a passport for Sara Dylan. Investigators returned to the house on Medgar Avenue with drills and shovels, convinced there might be bodies hidden beneath the floors or in the yard. Nothing turned up, but the sheer scale of the search showed how deeply they suspected Naso had kept some of his victims close.

Meanwhile, other teams combed through decades of cold cases, struggling against vague entries in the List of Ten and poorly preserved evidence from the 1970s.

Three months into his jail time, Naso was transferred to California custody. The move gave him hope. "California had better things to do than waste their time on me," he told me later. But the transfer came because investigators had caught a break: DNA tied him to a Marin County cold case—the 1977 murder of eighteen-year-old Roxene Roggasch.

Testing showed that the pantyhose used to strangle her belonged to Naso's wife, Judith, and another pair carried his DNA. From there, investigators tied him to three more murders: Carmen Colon, Pamela Parsons, and Tracy Tafoya.

On Monday, April 11, 2011, after nearly a year in custody for probation violations, Naso walked out of a California jail thinking he was free. At the gate, Detective Ryan Paterson stepped forward.

"Joseph Naso, you are under arrest for the murders of Roxene Roggasch, Carmen Colon, Pamela Parsons, and Tracy Tafoya."

Later, when I asked Naso about that moment, he laughed. "At first, I thought they wanted me for the guns I was selling. When the detective said I was under arrest for my girls, I figured I'd play it cool. There was no way they could tie me to their deaths. Too much time had gone by."

He smirked at his own cleverness. "They spent millions trying to figure it out. Millions! And they still got it wrong."

I reminded him he was on death row.

"Yeah, dumb luck," he said. "And they only figured out six. If I hadn't left my game around for them to find, they'd have nothing."

Not wanting me to have the last word, he grinned and added, "There's still twenty more girls out there. Naso twenty. Cops six. I still win."

31

Alphabet Murders

The day Joseph Naso was arrested, the headlines came fast—and so did the nicknames.

Because Naso's murders passed unnoticed for years, he never had one. Investigators never tied the bodies together, and his methods shifted—his modus operandi, or MO—leaving no consistent trail. His "signature," the private ritual that brought him satisfaction, remained invisible to police. And during the '60s through the '80s, investigators didn't yet have the forensic tools, psychological profiling, or media spotlight to connect him. He moved in the shadows, unseen.

The nicknames that finally emerged—"the Alphabet Killer," "the Double-Initial Killer"—along with certain so-called facts written about Joe, were false and misleading. Why these errors have never been corrected makes little sense, but the truth is different. Joseph Naso is a serial killer, but he isn't the Alphabet Killer or the Double-Initial Killer.

The same was true of "Crazy Joe." That name had nothing to do with his crimes. It was what some folks called him behind his back because he seemed a bit off, odd enough to come across strangely. The media lumped it in with the others, but it was never more than a neighborhood nickname.

The Rochester, New York, Alphabet murders haunted the public imagination—three young girls, all eleven or younger, raped, strangled, and dumped in towns matching their initials: Carmen Colon,

Wanda Walkowicz, Michelle Maenza. The coincidence was eerie, and confusion deepened when one of Naso's California victims also bore the name Carmen Colon.

When I finally asked him about it, Joe tilted his head. "Which ones?"

"The so-called Alphabet Murders," I said.

He shook his head, sharp and certain. "No. Those were children. I never touched a child. Never."

There was no hesitation in his voice. He wasn't lying. And later, DNA evidence proved him out—Naso was ruled out as the Rochester killer.

ALSO his story ABOUT THE DOUBLE INITIAL MURDERS OF 3 YOUNG GIRLS IN ROCHESTER IN 1973 IS ALL OUT OF CONTEX. Not CORRECT.

I LIVED IN OAKLAND FROM 1965 TO 1980. I VISITED N.Y. IN 1968 WITH MY FAMILY FOR 2 WEEKS. THEN IN 1976 I VISITED FAMILY ALONE FOR A WEEK OR SO.

IN 1973, I WAS AT THE TOP OF MY PROFESSION IN THE BAY AREA, TO BUSY TO EVEN VISIT GOLDEN GATE PARK. NEVER LEFT THE AREA. ALSO THE N.Y. STATE POLICE CONFIRMED IN 2011, I WAS DEFINATLY RULED OUT OF THE 1973 ROCHESTER INITIAL MURDERS. TAKE CARE.

I'LL SEE YOU WHEN I SEE YOU.

Note from Naso. He denied any involvement in the Double-Initial murders.

Still, the overlap was enough for many to draw conclusions, especially when four of the women Naso was convicted of killing—Roxene Roggasch, Carmen Colon, Pamela Parsons, and Tracy Tafoya—had names with matching initials.

It looked like coincidence. It wasn't.

When I pressed him, he finally admitted it. "It was my nod," he said, almost with pride. "My tribute to the Red-Light Bandit. Because he acknowledged me."

By "Red-Light Bandit," he meant Caryl Chessman, the notorious San Quentin inmate whose crimes and courtroom writings made him internationally famous before his execution in 1960. Naso had corresponded with Chessman, treasured the letters, and showed them off. Chessman had even invited Joe to attend his execution. The initials were Joe's tribute—C. C., Caryl Chessman.

Not every victim fit the pattern. Far from it. Joe killed plenty of women whose names had nothing to do with double initials. Some used street names, others gave him fake names, and often he didn't know their real ones until after they were dead. But when he found a woman whose initials matched, he seized on it. That was his nod to Chessman.

The obsession was real, and it wasn't his only one.

He also idolized Harvey Glatman, the "Lonely Hearts Killer," a photographer who lured women with modeling promises, bound and raped them, photographed them, strangled them, and dumped them in the desert. "Sound familiar?" Joe once said, smirking, as if daring me to connect the dots.

Unlike Glatman, Naso took years to evolve from rapist to murderer, but the influence was clear. Photography wasn't just a prop or a souvenir—it was the ritual the cops never recognized. For other killers, a photo might be a trophy, a way to hold on to a moment. For Joe, it was the act itself—the camera was his scalpel, the print his proof, the process his art.

And yet, at the very same time, he was capable of passing as respectable.

In 1977, just two months after he raped and murdered Roxene Roggasch, Naso was praised in writing by Donald A. Haight, vice president of San Francisco's Academy of Art College, where Joe worked as a photography instructor:

"Mr. Naso has been an instructor in the photography department from January 1977 to the present. I have found Mr. Naso totally dependable and extremely cooperative. He has an exceptional ability to work with new students who have little or no knowledge of photography. This can be a very difficult task for most professional photographers. Mr. Naso has managed extremely well."

Most accounts say Naso only studied at the Academy, but the truth is more telling: he was an instructor, respected and trusted. That normalcy was his camouflage.

And yet, photography wasn't just a disguise. It was his signature— the one thing he couldn't stop himself from doing. The photos were his trophies, his proof, the product of his twisted creativity. His art.

The media gave Joseph Naso nicknames in the end, but none captured the truth. Only one name fits.

The Portrait Killer.

32

The Trial

The trial of Joseph Naso opened in Marin County Superior Court, a case decades in the making. Reporters crowded the benches. Prospective jurors filled the room, thousands summoned over weeks of screening.

Naso insisted on representing himself—*in propria persona*. Judges warned him it was a mistake, especially in a death-penalty case, but he brushed them off. "I don't feel anyone knows this case as well as I do," he told the court. He boasted that he'd once served as a jury foreman. He wanted speed. He wanted control. Advisory counsel, public defender Pedro Oliveros, sat at his elbow, but Naso ignored him at every turn.

That arrogance carried straight into jury selection. Day after day, he questioned prospects himself, trying for charm but coming off as unsettling. At one point, he flailed his hands in the air, mocking prosecutor Rosemary Slote's gestures, then turned to the panel. "I was watching you," he said, laughing at his own joke. The jurors didn't laugh.

He pressed on, asking what they thought of him and assuring them it was fine to be blunt. "Don't worry," he said. "You won't hurt my feelings."

One prospect didn't hesitate: "I don't like you."

Another called him "weird, creepy, and scary."

A woman told him his mocking of the prosecutor was "objectionable."

It was the jury's first glimpse of the man who would be defending himself. And it wasn't promising.

When testimony began, the prosecution wasted no time. The jurors saw photographs of bodies: roadside dirt, pantyhose knotted and stuffed. Gasps rose from the gallery, and at least one juror wiped away tears.

Naso, seventy-nine years old, rose in a dark suit and glasses, a blue tie at his throat, and told the jury he had "been waiting two years and two months" to speak. He said he wasn't the monster they'd heard about. He showed childhood photos. He called his pictures "art," his models willing.

Across the room, Rosemary Slote waited, calm and patient. She called him what the evidence showed: a serial rapist and murderer.

The journal became the centerpiece. Slote read it aloud, the language plain and ugly:

"Girl in North Buffalo woods. She was real pretty. Had to knock her out first."

"Rochester 1958 . . . I forced her down on the back seat. She was scared."

"Berkeley Hills, 1961 . . . picked up a girl and raped her in the car."

"London . . . outside the front door I overpowered her and ravaged her. I couldn't help myself."

Naso brushed it off. Loose talk, he said. "I picked up a broad and I raped her" was just his phrase for good sex. He winked at the jurors, trying for humor, and begged them to ignore what was printed in his own hand.

But the journal wasn't the only record.

5) - GIRL IN NORTH BUFFALO WOODS. SHE WAS REAL PROWL. FIGHT. SEAT OF MY CAR. HAD TO KNOCK HER OUT FIRST. 1968

6) - GIRL IN BUFFALO, I PICKED UP HITCHING. SHE HAD NO TEETH. SHE SMELLED. GAVE ME A GOOD BJ.

7) PAST HERR - TONAWANDA) A VERY NICE I BURIED HER OFTEN. NICE GIRL. I DID HER WRONG. I'M SORRY. WE WERE ENGAGED.

8) - BUFFALO GIRL I PICKED UP IN COLONIAL PLACE ON MAIN ST. SHE WAS ONLY 17. I TOOK HER UP TO A HOTEL ROOM. GOT HER DRUNK. SHE HAD HER PERIOD. PERIOD OUT. I PUT IT IN HER (ANAL). PICKED HER UP AFTER WORK ONCE. AND PUT IT TO HER IN THE FRONT SEAT. SHE TOLD HER MOTHER. HER MOTHER TOLD COPS. (OP. (DETECTIVE) TOLD ME TO GET OUT OF TOWN. 1958

15) SOPHIA-KANSAS GIRL I FOLLOWED AND MET AT TRAD ASHLEY. DON'T SHARE. SHE WAS GEORGINE. GREED LEG IN NYLON, HALL. HAD TO RAPE HER IN MY (CAR ON A COLD WINTERY NIGHT SNOW STORM - (47 PROBABLY)

16) - KANSAS CITY - GIRL I PICKED UP AND TOOK HER OUT IN WOODS NORTH OF CITY AND HAD TO RAPE-HER ON THE GROUND

17) - KANSAS CITY - GIRL I MET ON THE BUS GOING TO LOMPOC CITY FROM WICHITA. SHE WAS ENGAGED AND REAL KNOCKOUT. HAD A ICE-CREAM SODA WITH HER AT ICAFE DRUGSTORF. I TAPED. TOOK UP TO A MOTEL ROOM AND GAVE HER A REAL GOOD SCREW. ONE OF MY NICEST AFFAIRS.

18) - TORONTO, CANADA - VERY PRETTY GIRL I PICKED UP AT DANCE. DROVE HER TO THE OUTSKIRTS AND PULLED OVER TO SIDE OF ROAD. HAD TO FORCE HER ON THE FRONT SEAT. SHE CALLED BUT I DIDN'T. I LOVED IT. COME IN HER. SHE WORRIED ABOUT BEING PREGNANT.

19) 14 YR OLD GIRL I FINGERED IN THE BACK SEAT OF A GREYHOUND BUS IN KANSAS. (WICHITA TO SALINA RUN)

6)

Excerpt from Naso's *Rape Journal*.

The List of Ten seemed cryptic on its face—until the prosecution laid it beside DNA, photographs, clippings, bank contents, and his calendar:

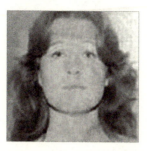

Roxene Roggasch (1977)

Eighteen. Found strangled near Lagunitas Road. The list: "Girl near Loganitas." His spelling was off, but the DNA on her body matched Naso, and pantyhose used in the murder carried his ex-wife's DNA. Because the killing occurred before California reinstated the death penalty in 1978, the charge carried life without parole.

Carmen Colon (1978)

Twenty-two. Found along the Carquinez Scenic Highway near Port Costa. The list: "Girl near Port Costa." DNA beneath her fingernails was consistent with Naso's. Jurors saw the words on his list as confirmation of what the evidence suggested.

Pamela Parsons (1993)

Thirty-eight. Dumped near Linda, Yuba County—minutes from where Naso lived. The list: "Girl from Linda (Yuba County)." In his safe-deposit box, investigators found photographs of Pamela in lingerie taken in his home, laminated clippings about her murder and her obituary, and $152,400 in cash. On his calendar, the entry for September 15 read: "Stayed in Yuba City all day long. Took care of some old business." It was the last day she was seen alive. Four days later, her body was found.

Tracy Tafoya (1994)

Thirty-one. Found in a ditch by the Marysville Cemetery, off Highway 70. The list: "Girl from MRSV (cemetery)." In his property were photographs of her in lingerie her husband recognized as gifts he'd bought—photos in which the woman was missing most of a finger, as Tracy was. On his calendar, the entry for August 6 read: "Picked up a nice broad in Marysville. 4 p.m. She came over for four hours. Took photographs. Nice legs. She ripped me off." It was the last day she was known to be alive.

On August 20, 2013, after roughly eight hours of deliberation, the jury found him guilty of four counts of first-degree murder and the special circumstance of multiple murders.

During the penalty phase, death or life without parole were the choices now. The state introduced more of his life, and more of his dead:

Sharieea Patton (1981)

Fifty-six. Strangled in 1981 near the Tiburon shore. The list: "Lady from 839 Leavenworth"—her San Francisco address, where Naso managed the building. In his possession was a photograph of a woman wearing a gray rabbit-fur coat. Her daughter testified the coat was her mother's.

Sara Dylan (born Rene Shapiro, 1992)

Thirty-one. A Bob Dylan devotee who vanished in 1992 while following the tour. She had legally changed her name to Sara Dylan—the name of Dylan's first wife—and carried a Dylan pin everywhere. The list: "Girl in Woodland (near Nevada County)." Her skull was discovered in 2004 in the Tahoe National Forest. In Naso's safe-deposit box were her passport and the Dylan pin. For years he referred to her only as Sara Dylan, convinced of a connection to the singer. It wasn't until trial that he—and the jury—heard her birth name: Rene Shapiro.

Naso tried to humanize himself. He called his ex-wife to talk about Cub Scouts, Little League, fatherhood. He asked if she wanted him to live. She said yes—and still the ledger of his crimes outweighed the plea. The jury returned swiftly with a recommendation of death.

On November 22, 2013, Judge Andrew Sweet imposed sentence. For Roggasch—murder committed before California reinstated capital punishment—life without the possibility of parole. For Colon, Parsons, and Tafoya—death, consecutive.

The judge's words cut through the hush: the murders were vicious, brutal, driven by sexual motive, planned and deliberate—inflicting an "abhorrent degree of suffering and indignity." Naso, he said, was a "pathological predator and cold-blooded killer," the kind that haunts parents and makes strangers turn away. And he had shown no remorse whatsoever.

Victims' families spoke. A daughter who did not want him executed but wanted him to suffer what he had made them suffer. A son who said his childhood had been stolen and wished Naso a very long life to feel it.

When it was his turn, Naso told the court he felt sorry for the victims and their families. "I have remorse for anyone who dies in a violent manner and for their families," he said, "but I'm not guilty of these crimes."

He registered little on his face when the verdicts were first read. He revealed nothing now that mattered. At seventy-nine, he entered death row as the oldest prisoner ever condemned in California.

When the sentence was read, the courtroom closed the book on Joseph Naso. But in San Quentin, the story was far from over. Conversations weren't enough anymore. If the truth was going to survive the yard and the years, I had to get it on paper—something I could place in the hands of law enforcement.

The chance came suddenly. I took it.

PART THREE

THE CLOSURE

Four of Naso's cold cases I was able to help solve. *Clockwise from upper left*: Lynn Ruth Connes, Charlotte Cook, Pamela Lambson, and Rebecca Jean Dunn.

33

The Confession

In the case of *The People v. Joseph Naso*, the people dropped the ball. Prosecutors love death sentences because they look like victories. They get their headlines, their chest-beating moment, their trophies for the wall. But in California, death row isn't punishment. It's protection. A private cell, stipends, canteen privileges, packages of food and electronics. And for men like Joe, it's even worse—it's celebrity.

The state has executed only a handful of inmates since the sixties, but killers like Naso rarely understand that. To them, death sentence means the needle. If law enforcement had dangled a deal—life without parole instead of death—in exchange for the truth, Joe would've jumped. And a lot of unanswered murders could have been solved.

I know this because I tested it myself.

It started in 2020. Joe shuffled up to me on the yard, his voice low, his eyes nervous.

"Bill, do you know anything about the governor giving pardons to people?"

"People in prison don't get pardons," I told him. "They get commutations. You have to be released first to get a pardon."

"Yeah, yeah, yeah." He brushed me off with a flick of his hand. "But do you know how to do it?"

"Yeah, sure. I've actually already done it."

His eyes narrowed. "What are you talking about? Who did it for you?"

"I did it with my attorney."

He gave me a sideways look, suspicion written all over his face. "Right."

Joe's angle was clear. He wasn't dreaming about walking free; he wanted out of San Quentin. Off death row. Into a facility where life was more comfortable, where he'd feel safer from the predators who circled men like him. And more than that, he wanted to be closer to his son, to make visits possible. That was the fantasy he clung to, the prize he thought the governor might grant him.

That's when the idea hit me. "I've got a friend," I said. "Walt. He's a lead writer at *Forbes*, a man with a reputation. The first Saturday of every month, he golfs with Governor Newsom. Big deals get made on golf courses, Joe. You know that."

Walt was real—a respected journalist, a man I knew and trusted. But the golf-with-Newsom part? That was pure fiction, tailored for Joe. He'd bragged about his caddie days back east, watching power brokers cut deals on the greens. I gave him a story he couldn't resist.

He shifted closer, hungry. "Do you talk to Walt a lot? Can you talk to him about me?"

"Not empty-handed," I said. "I can't go to him and say, 'Let's talk about my buddy Joe, the serial killer.' You've got to give me something tangible. The governor will be reluctant to give a serial killer a commutation, and there are still murders the cops think you committed. The governor will know that."

His eyes locked on mine, searching.

I pressed harder. "You have information you can trade for your freedom."

That's when it cracked him open. His face collapsed, and to my surprise, tears spilled. "I'll do it. I'll tell where they're at. I'm sorry. I'm not a threat to anyone anymore. All that's in the past. I'm an old man."

I knew better. But I also knew I had him.

ON FRIDAY, WE CAN TALK IN THAT SAME
CORNER. OR THE OTHER FRONT CORNER.
BUT WATCH OUT FOR SNOOPY INMATES
LIKE BILL SUPP AND WEAVER.

                    P.S.

WHEN I WAS A BOY, I WAS A CHAMPION
CADDY AT A PROMINENT PRESTEGOUS N.Y.
COUNTRY CLUB, I WAS PAID $3.00 FOR
9 HOLES DOUBLES. AND 6.00 FOR 18 HOLES DOUBLES
I WAS A FAVORITY CADDY FOR SOME VERY WEALTHY
AND HIGH RANKING MEMBERS. (TIPS WERE GOOD) BUT, I
LEARNED ALOT BY LISTENING TO THEIR CHATTER, WHILE
THEY PLAYED. THINGS LIKE, I'LL GIVE YOU 10 GAS
STATIONS FOR 3 OF YOUR 4 STAR HOTELS. THE REASON
I TELL YOU, IS BIG PEOPLE MAKE BIG DEALS,
NOT IN THE OFFICE. BUT ON THE GOLF COARSE.
WHERE ITS QUIET AND PRIVATE.

                    SO LONG; Joe
WHAT ABOUT HIS PHONE NO. ?

Naso's note: making big deals on the golf course.

The next day, I played my advantage. I pulled out a copy of the court order that had once reversed my conviction—careful not to mention that the decision was already under appeal and could soon be reinstated.

Joe studied the document, his face shifting from doubt to awe. To him, it was proof: I had real connections, maybe even the kind that could reach all the way to the governor's office.

That sealed it.

"What do you need from me?" he asked.

"You have to give me something in good faith," I told him. "You've denied everything. You have to take responsibility and give them something—like the location and description of a girl they don't know about. How you killed her."

"But I've told you. I've given you the information."

"Joe, I'm not the one who can do it. I'm a nobody. That's hearsay. You have to write it."

He twisted his hands together, anxious. "Why can't they just come see me?"

"No. They aren't gonna come see you. You have to get their attention. The only way this works is if you put it on paper. A written confession—something real they can't ignore."

I had to get him to write it down. I was so close I could taste it. Like a fat, hungry kid in a candy store, I could already feel the sugar rush of his confession.

"If you want this to work, you have to write it down, and I'll give it to Walt."

I had to be careful. I made him promise not to tell a soul about our plan. Not one word. Because if anyone else caught wind of it, they wouldn't just know it was total bullshit—they'd come after me for being a snitch. And in here, that's a death sentence of its own.

He came back a couple of times and said, "Are you sure this is what I need to do? Give me Walt's number and I'll call him."

MAY 19-2020

Bill,
ON MON. I TALKED TO MAURICE
THROUGH THE FENCE MOSTLY ABOUT THE
PILOT PROGRAM, AND MY INTEREST IN GOING TO
THE MED. FACILITY AT VACCAVILLE. I GO TO
COMMITTEE IN NOV. I DID NOT GO INTO ANY
DETAILS ABOUT A PARDON AND MY APPLICATION
TO NEWSOM. I ONLY SAID I WISH I COULD
GET A PARDON. BUT IT ALL WENT OVER HIS HEAD,
AND I'M SURE HE WILL NOT LOSE ANY SLEEP
ON IT. HE, NOR ANY OTHER INMATE
KNOWS ANYTHING ABOUT WHAT YOU AND I
TALK ABOUT. WHAT YOU AND I TALK ABOUT
IS KEPT BETWEEN YOU AND ME.

Naso's note: not talking with other inmates.

"No, it doesn't work like that," I told him. "I'm not going to give you the number of a prestigious writer, for God's sake, so you can run a game on him. This is all or nothing."

I refused. Instead, I gave him Walt's mailing address—just enough truth to make the lie unshakable. Then I called Walt on the outside.

"Joe's probably going to write to you," I said. "String him along if you have to. I'm close to getting a confession on paper."

Finally, one morning, Joe slipped me a folded page.

"I've written everything I can remember," he said. "You don't have to ask me any more questions."

I stared at it, shocked. I never thought he'd actually do it. But there it was in my hands: his confession to killing the girl from Berkeley.

A single sheet, all caps from start to finish:

I SAW A GIRL'S AD, TO MODEL, IN THE BERKELEY BARB. . . .
SHE WOULD RIDE BIKE. . . . DURING THIS SESSION, I CHOKED
HER TO DEATH. NO VIOLENCE. NO SEX. JUST A QUICK
DEATH. . . . TO THIS DAY, I HAVE ALWAYS FELT MUCH RE-
GRET AND SORROW FOR THIS TERRIBLE ACT.

His words sprawled across the page in block letters, cold and clini-
cal. Even his "regret and sorrow" at the end rang hollow. I'd spent too
many hours listening to him brag, justify, and arouse himself with
these stories to believe otherwise.

Almost immediately, he panicked.
"I want it back. Give it back."
"I can't. I already gave it to Walt. It's out there."
"Then have him destroy it!"
"The best I can do is tell him to burn it. If it comes back through
the mail, the cops will see it and you'll be finished."
Weeks later, I told him it was destroyed. "No one's come for you,
Joe. If the cops had seen it, they'd already be all over you."
His shoulders sagged with relief. On the surface, we slipped back
into our routine. But everything had changed.
That single page proved what I'd been saying all along: if you dangle
the illusion of freedom, a serial killer will finally confess.
But the words themselves meant nothing. Joe's regret was a per-
formance, nothing more than another mask. What drove him wasn't
remorse—it was desperation.
And in that desperation, Joseph Naso finally wrote down what he
had hidden for half a century—his confession to killing the girl from
Berkeley.

THE GIRL FROM BERKELEY

IT WAS SOMETIME IN THE LATE 1960's UP TO THE MID 70's THAT I SAW A GIRL'S AD. TO MODEL, IN THE BERKELEY BARB TABLOID. I CALLED HER. AND WE MADE A DATE TO MEET IN DOWNTOWN BERK. SHE SAID SHE WOULD RIDE BIKE TO A CERTAIN LOCATION, AT A CERTAIN TIME. WE MET. AFTER SHE CHAINED HER BIKE, I DROVE HER TO MY HOME IN OAKLAND. I WOULD BE AT HOME ALONE AT THAT TIME OF DAY. ONCE INSIDE, WE TALKED A BIT TO GET AQUAINTED. SHE WAS NICE LOOKING, WITH LONG BROWN HAIR AND SEEMED TO HAVE A GOOD FIGURE I'D GUESS ABOUT 5'4" AND 120 LB. SHE GAVE ME HER NAME, AND SAID SHE WAS ORIG. FROM N.Y. CITY. I DIDN'T PLAN ON DATING HER. SO I DID NOT CONCENTRATE ON HER NAME AND DON'T RECALL IT. SHE SAID SHE DID NUDE MODELING. BUT I SAID I WAS ONLY INTERESTED IN NO MORE THAN TOPLESS PORTRAITS. WE AGREED ON A FEE. SHE WAS EASY TO WORK WITH. I HAD HER LAY ON HER BACK ON MY SOFA FOR SOME TOPLESS SHOTS. DURING THIS SESSION I CHOKED HER TO DEATH. NO VIOLENCE. NO SEX. JUST A QUICK DEATH. I PUT HER IN TRASH BAG AND IN MY CAR TRUNK. LATE THAT NIGHT, I DROVE OVER THE RICHMOND-SAN RAFAEL BRIDGE, AND IN THE LOW RAIL SECTION I STOPPED AND QUICKLY PUT THE BAG OVER INTO THE BAY. IT WASN'T EASY BUT BACK THEN I HAD THE VIGOR. TO THIS DAY, I HAVE ALWAYS FELT MUCH REGRET AND SORROW FOR THIS TERRIBLE ACT. I WOULD THINK THE BERKELEY P.D. HAVE A RECORD OF A MISSING GIRL, BACK THEN, WHO MADE A DATE TO RIDE HER BIKE TO MEET SOMEONE AND VANISHED.

Naso's confession: The Girl from Berkeley.

34

The Rat

With Naso's confession in hand, I knew I couldn't sit still. The list of unsolved murders was bigger than me, and if I wanted to bring answers to the victims' families, I needed help from the outside.

But who could I trust? If I went to law enforcement, the whole thing would leak. One headline and it would be all over East Block. The label would stick to me forever—snitch—and I wouldn't last a week.

So I turned to private investigators. I wrote letter after letter, sometimes slipping them into the outgoing mail with a surge of hope, sometimes calling the numbers I found, even though I knew the odds. Most never answered. The few who did made it clear: retainer required. Prices I could never pay.

Still, I kept writing. Six investigators became ten, then sixteen. I told myself someone would take the work on principle, for the sake of finalizing the cases and giving the families some closure.

But the truth was brutal: weeks passed, and no one wrote back. I was on my own.

That didn't mean I stopped. I began shaping chapters, setting down the stories Naso had given me and the way he'd given them—his arrogance, his contempt, his casual cruelty. If no one else would investigate, the book itself would have to become the record. Each page I filled felt like a weapon: one more safeguard against his secrets being buried with him.

take my calls. No answer from letters
I wrote. Frustrating no one will help
unless I pay thousands.

Will keep investigating. Doing everything
I can. - I'm on my own.

Still no investigator. Written 16.
All require retainer to investigate. Can't
afford their prices.

If I go to law enforcement. They'll
leak it to press. It will be all over
death row - I'll be killed. - Need
a plan to get a Real investigator

My journal: reaching out to investigators.

While the outside world ignored my letters, inside San Quentin men were dying all around me.

The year 2020 had cut through this place as brutally as it had the world outside. On death row, COVID-19 claimed more men than the execution chamber had since 1967. Younger, stronger convicts were falling fast.

I kept waiting for the day the sirens would wail for cell 1-EB-80, announcing that Joseph Naso had finally gone down. Old. Frail. Weak. He was the perfect target for the virus.

But he slipped past it. I spotted him one morning shuffling across the ADA yard, one of the few to venture out while so many others coughed in their cells. That's when it hit me: this guy's a cockroach. It would take a nuclear blast to kill him. The same man who had sent women to their graves seemed immune to the thing cutting through us.

In June 2021, old scores were coming due. June marked hunting season on the yards, when violence always erupted. I'd seen it year after year—knives settling disputes, grudges paid in blood.

By then my assignment as IDAP worker was over. I'd spent years on the ADA yard, pushing wheelchairs, studying the predators who pretended to be harmless. But that was done. I was back in my regular yard, separated from the ADA yard by a chain-link fence.

It had only been a week since my last day there when I felt the shift.

The sun pressed down, heat bouncing off the concrete. I'd just finished a set of jump squats when the air changed. You learn to feel it in here—the hush that rolls through before the storm. My eyes swept yard six and the others, one by one. Nothing out of place. Card games. Workouts. Deals through the fence. All routine.

Then my gaze locked on the ADA yard.

Rockhead was at the fence, distracted, passing something to a guy from yard four. He didn't see the old man limping toward him—Blue, new to the yard, moving with purpose.

My eyes slid to the opposite yard and confirmed what I suspected: Rockhead's former crew was watching. If they were paying that much attention, it could only mean they'd learned the truth—Rockhead was a snitch. And there would be only one outcome.

Steel flashed. Blue's left hand clamped Rockhead's shirt. His right hand drove the shank in—chest, throat, ribs. Over and over. Rockhead twisted and broke loose, but he was already bleeding out.

Blue was older, weaker, but the weapon evened the odds. If it came from Rider, Rockhead's old shot-caller, it was built for one purpose only: to kill.

Before the gunner even registered what had happened, the knife was gone, passed clean through the fence to the same man Rockhead had been talking with. That was the proof. Rockhead had been set up. Nothing in prison happens by accident. Every move has other men behind it.

Finally, the whistle shrieked. "Down!" the gunner shouted.

Every man dropped.

Every man but Joseph Naso.

He stood tall in the open, pointing. His voice carried over the alarm. "Don't shoot—it wasn't me! It was him. He stabbed him and passed the knife to that guy!" He jabbed his finger from Blue to the man on the other side of the fence.

As the siren blared, the words rippled yard to yard.

"Fuckin' rat."

When the alarm finally cut off, the yards stayed frozen under the gunner's eye. Medics rushed Rockhead out, blood pooling beneath the stretcher. Slowly, activity picked up again as if nothing had happened.

But something had happened. Everyone had seen it. Naso, standing tall, pointing fingers in front of God and country. The verdict was already written, stamped on him for life.

I went back to my workout, trying to shake the image. That's when Ghost approached.

"You got a minute?" he asked.

I nodded. We fell into step along the edge of the basketball court, the fence on one side, the hot wall on the other.

Ghost didn't waste words. When he spoke, it mattered. He was still one of the most powerful men on the yard, and nothing happened here without his knowledge.

"What's your angle on that piece of shit rat who told on Blue?" he asked finally. His tone was calm, but the weight behind it was clear. "I know you protected him from Rockhead before. But I know you don't do anything without a reason."

I took my time before answering. Respect demanded I give it to him straight.

"My interest in Naso isn't about him," I said. "It's about information. He's a serial killer. I want his story."

Ghost walked a few more paces in silence, then gave a single look of acknowledgment. "You're lucky you said that," he said. "If you'd fed me some bullshit, he'd be gone already. I had it lined up."

We walked another lap. Ghost gave a low laugh. "Man, I don't know how you do it—spending years talking to a motherfucker like that. I'd have gutted him already."

"Believe me, sometimes it takes everything I have not to strangle him on the spot."

He stopped and offered his hand. "I'll let you get back to it. Just wanted to know where you stood."

We shook. Then he walked off.

I picked up my workout where I'd left off, but the thought kept circling: Naso had made it harder than ever for me to stay close to him. He was a known rat now, and my association with him was poison. Especially if he'd been noticed by someone like Ghost.

His words—and my own thoughts—stayed with me long after I left the yard. He had given me room to keep working Naso, but I knew it wouldn't last forever. My cover was fragile. The minute Ghost was gone, so was my protection.

Back in my cell that night, I opened my notebook. The pages were filling up—Naso's words, his confessions, the fragments of his past. Piece by piece, they were becoming the chapters of the book I hoped someone would one day carry forward.

But I couldn't escape the truth: outside these walls, no one was coming to help me. And inside, I was tied to a man everyone now wanted dead.

And hanging over me was my own uncertainty. I was still waiting on a ruling from the Ninth Circuit. Until that came, my future was as unsettled as Naso's.

The storm was closing in, from every direction.

—⁓—

For the next ten days, the ADA yard was on lockdown, as always after a stabbing that brutal. When the gates finally opened, I expected Naso to show himself. He didn't. Not the first day, not the second, not the third. Maybe he'd had a rare moment of clarity—realizing what he'd done and fearing the consequences.

I wasn't the only one who noticed.

About a week later, when Naso still hadn't come out, Ghost remarked in passing, "Looks like your boy may have second thoughts about his safety after that move he pulled."

Maybe he was right.

35

Coward's Heart

After ratting on Blue, Naso stayed hidden—until one morning just past four.

I'd been sipping a cup of coffee, settling into the ritual that had kept me alive for decades: listening.

Every man on death row has his patterns. A cough at the same hour. The scrape of shoes down the tier. The clang of a toilet flushing right before dawn. If you learn the rhythms, you also learn when something breaks them. And a broken rhythm can mean the difference between living and dying.

The night watchman was making his rounds, his baton knocking lightly against his thigh with each step. I tracked him in my mind as he moved down the first tier. He passed cell 77, then paused.

"Are you okay?" I heard him call out. "Can you stand?"

A second later the alarm blared, and boots hammered the floor above and below me.

"Naso, can you hear me?" the guard shouted. "Come to the bars."

At the mention of his name, I focused. Cell 80.

The noise swelled—doors opening, voices echoing. EMTs rushed in, their commands clipped and urgent. I couldn't see much, but I could hear them working over him. Chest compressions. The hiss of oxygen. Then the heavy scrape of the gurney as they hauled him out.

For long minutes the alarm screamed through the block. Then it cut off as suddenly as it had started, leaving only the echo of running boots and the knowledge of what I had just witnessed: Joseph Naso, the man who had once strangled women without hesitation, laid out and fighting for his life on the floor of San Quentin.

They rushed him through the gates and into an ambulance waiting outside the prison. Surgeons would cut him open, slide stents into his arteries, and fight to give him more time.

That was the part that stopped me cold. The State of California had already sentenced him to die. Every man on death row knew what he was, and they wanted him gone too. Yet when his heart failed, the system bent over backward to save him.

His victims never got that chance. They begged for breath with his hands around their throats, and he gave them none. But here he was—old, frail, evil—and every resource was spent to drag him back.

It was hypocrisy and irony and another reminder of how upside down this place could be.

About a month later, Naso was back. Two stents in his chest, a little paler, but still shuffling across the ADA yard as if nothing had happened. I watched him closely, curious to see how the others would respond.

It didn't take long.

The first to make his feelings known was David Carpenter, the Trailside Killer. Carpenter was over ninety, stooped and frail, but when Naso wandered too close, he snarled, "Get the hell away from me, you stool pigeon. Don't come anywhere near me."

He rose with his cane in both hands. "I'll smash your fuckin' skull to pieces!"

Naso, caught off guard, backed away quickly—only to run into worse. Beetle, another serial killer, spat straight into his face. "Rat."

The word cut deeper than the spit. On the ADA yard, where most men were old and broken down, it was unlikely anyone would risk another stabbing over Naso. But the display mattered. It was a verdict, delivered in public. Carpenter with his cane, Beetle with his spit. Both of them announcing for everyone to see: Naso was filth.

For him, it was humiliation. For me, it was confirmation. The code of prison life had closed in on him, and there was no crawling back.

Soon after, he came looking for me. I saw him waving from the fence line, his eyes darting like a cornered animal.

"Did you see that?" he blurted before I said a word. "He spit in my face! If I had a gun, I'd shoot him right between the eyes."

I kept my voice even. "I saw."

"I need you to help me," he said. "I'll pay you three thousand dollars. Have somebody work him over."

I stepped closer, lowering my tone so only he could hear. "Joe, I'm not your errand boy. You ratted on Blue in front of everybody. You're lucky no one slit your skinny throat. Somebody spitting in your face is the least of your problems."

He blinked at me, refusing to take it in. "Yeah, but he disrespected me."

That was it. I stepped in closer. "You're starting to piss me off, Joe. You love killing, but only when your victims can't fight back. Now's your chance to be the big bad man you pretend to be. Go over there, grab Beetle's cane, and smash it over his head. That's how you earn respect."

We both knew he wouldn't. Joseph Naso was all menace when the odds were tilted, but face him against men who could stand their ground, and he folded. Out here, he was nothing but a coward.

I turned and walked away, leaving him stewing in the corner. The isolation was what I wanted. Desperation would bring him back, and when it did, I'd make sure it was on my terms.

For more than a week I ignored him. He lingered at the fence, watching me, waiting for a signal, but I gave him nothing. The silence wore on him, the way I knew it would.

Finally, with a couple of hours left before they called us in from the yard, I glanced his way. He jumped on it instantly, waving me over.

"What's up, Joe?" I asked. "What's going on in your mind?"

"Nothing," he said too quickly. "Just wanted to talk. You know, we never talk."

I let him stew a moment, then said, "Certain things happened that made it smarter to keep my distance."

That pricked him. "Let's not talk about that anymore, okay? Did you know I had a heart attack? They put two stents in me. I feel great now."

"I heard," I said. "Glad you're on your feet. But you haven't answered the real question. Why did you tell on Blue? And worse—why did you do it in front of everyone?"

He dodged, gave excuses, shifted blame, but it all came back to the same thing: himself. Then he cut to what really mattered to him. "So, Bill, you think any of these guys will try to hurt me?"

I decided it was time to tighten the screws. "I don't think the danger's in your yard," I told him. "It's from the others. I've already heard talk—one crew planning to spear you through the gate, another planning poison."

His eyes flicked sideways, trying to gauge if I was serious. "Can you talk to them? I can pay them. Or pay you."

"I don't want your money. What I want is for you to keep your mouth shut. That's what gets you in trouble. You stop running to the cops, and I'll do what I can."

Relief washed over his face. "That's great. I won't say anything anymore."

"Good," I said. "Do that, and maybe you'll live a little longer."

36

Lynn Ruth Connes

Naso survived. He kept his mouth shut, just as I'd warned him to, and for the moment, that was enough. The games with him continued, but my own life was shifting. Courts, lawyers, and judges were deciding what came next for me.

By October 2021, the Ninth Circuit had reversed part of the District Court's ruling. My conviction was reinstated, but the penalty phase reversal stood. In short, my guilt was affirmed, but my death sentence was gone.

A month later, the Orange County District Attorney announced he would not seek death again. I would serve the rest of my life in prison.

Then, in December, I postponed my sentencing hearing for a year. I needed time—time on death row to pull more truth from Joseph Naso, and time to finally learn the identity of the girl he had confessed to killing in Berkeley. Some would say—I know many would say—I was crazy to deliberately delay my sentencing and transfer from San Quentin just to finish this book. But for me, it was more than a book. It was about finishing a job I had started, a vow to do everything I could to bring justice to Naso's victims. To others, that choice was impossible to understand.

Seven months later, in July 2022, I was watching *The Hunt for the Zodiac Killer* on Story Television. Former FBI agent Ken Mains co-starred in the series, and something in his presence stopped me. It was his sincerity, his conviction that truth mattered. That's what I needed—someone who cared about the truth as much as I did.

I asked Matt Ralston, the co-host of my *Death Row Diaries* true-crime podcast, to reach out to him. To my surprise, Mains responded immediately. Within weeks, he had my manuscript, Naso's handwritten confession about the "girl from Berkeley," and the photographs that accompanied it.

The details made Mains's task straightforward. He queried the NamUs missing-persons database for young women who had vanished in the '60s and '70s, leaving a bicycle chained outside a restaurant in Berkeley. One case matched perfectly: Lynn Ruth Connes, twenty years old. She had disappeared on May 20, 1976, after arranging to meet a photographer who responded to an ad she had placed in the *Berkeley Barb*. Her bicycle was later found chained outside the Bateau Ivre restaurant on Telegraph Avenue. Lynn's body was never found.

Before he would tell Berkeley Police the case was solved, Mains wanted one more piece of confirmation. He printed out two photographs of Connes—a freckle-faced young woman with dark blond hair parted in the middle, a faint scar on her lower lip—and sent them to me with a request: observe Naso's reaction.

On August 5, 2022, I walked to the chain-link fence separating my yard from the ADA yard, two photographs of Lynn tucked in the waistband of my shorts. Naso spotted me and shuffled over.

"Hey, Bill," he said casually. "You see the Raiders play in the Hall of Fame Game?"

I studied him. Ten years had withered him. "No, I didn't. But I've got something else. Pictures of a young lady. Maybe you know her."

His eyebrows shot up. "Oh yeah? You got them on you? Let me see."

"They're right here." I pulled the envelope free and slipped it through the fence.

He tore it open, pulled out the two photographs, and froze. His whole body stilled, his face slackening as if the world around him had gone silent. Then his hand rose, trembling, and he touched the pictures—caressing the young woman's face with the gentleness of a lover.

Lynn Ruth Connes: The Girl
from Berkeley.

He looked up at me, his eyes suddenly sharp. "How did you find her?"

"I told you before. I have friends in both high and low places."

He nodded slowly, still staring at the images. "Can I keep them?"

"I don't know, Joe," I said evenly. "Or should I call you Jeff?"

A smile crept over his lips.

"Why do you want them?" I asked. "I figured you'd forgotten her."

He shook his head, eyes locked on the photographs. "I never forget one of my girls. She was one of the special ones. The girl from Berkeley."

For the first time, it felt like it had all been worth it—the years of maneuvering, the risks I took to stay close to him. Naso had provided what investigators never could: the chance to bring closure to a family. At last, one of the faceless victims on his list had a name.

37

Final Days on Death Row

By December 2022, I knew I was on borrowed time. Not only had I been working with Ken Mains, a fact that could get me killed if word spread, but Ghost had been transferred. So I asked my attorney to schedule my sentencing hearing.

On January 27, 2023, at 10 a.m., I was escorted in handcuffs, waist chains, and leg irons to the San Quentin video courtroom and seated in front of a large monitor. Within seconds, my attorney appeared on screen: Orange County Public Defender Andrew Nechaev.

"Good morning, William. Can you hear and see me clearly?"

"Yes."

"How do you feel? Any questions?"

"No questions. But I do have a request."

He fixed his eyes on me. "What is it?"

"I'd like to address the court—and the district attorney."

He nodded. "I'll let the judge know."

Moments later the judge appeared, sat down behind the bench, and shuffled his papers. His voice was calm, but the weight of the moment pressed on me heavier than the chains around my waist.

"Good morning, Mr. Noguera. I see we are here to reduce your sentence from death to life without parole. Are the People ready to proceed?" he asked, looking at the district attorney.

"The People are ready, Your Honor."

The judge turned to Andrew. "Any motions before we proceed?"

"Only one, Judge. Mr. Noguera would like to address the court."

The judge studied me. "Mr. Noguera, I'm sure your attorney would advise against making statements. Do you still wish to speak?"

"Yes, Your Honor."

"All right. Proceed."

I took a deep breath. The courtroom was so quiet I could hear the faint buzz of the monitor. "First, I'd like to apologize to the people of Orange County for my actions. I take full responsibility for the decision I made over forty years ago to take a human life. I also apologize to the court for the resources spent on me—resources that could have served the community instead. For that, I'm sorry."

After a pause, the judge said, "Thank you, Mr. Noguera. If all parties are prepared, I'll enter the sentence."

I sat there cuffed and chained, hearing the words but drifting back to the teenager I'd been in 1983—the boy who killed Jovita Navarro. Not for greed or money, and not because he was evil. He killed for love. For the love of his unborn child, murdered through abortion at eighteen weeks. He killed to protect the mother of that child, a girl Jovita had abused since she was nine. Those memories rushed in—sharp, relentless.

"I sentence you to life in prison without the possibility of parole," the judge said, pulling me back. In less than a minute, he'd undone what a jury decided over forty years ago.

"Good luck to you, Mr. Noguera."

The same words another judge had spoken when he sentenced me to death. My jaw clenched.

There were no reporters, no cameras, none of the drama from the first time when it was front-page news—the youngest person in Orange County sentenced to death. Now the courtroom was only flickering screens and muted voices. This time I was simply escorted back to my cell on death row to await paperwork, which would take weeks. Meanwhile, nothing changed. I still lived in cell 77 on the fourth tier of East Block, surrounded by killers.

That is, until something did.

On February 19, 2023, during meditation, I felt it. A shift, subtle but undeniable. After decades of relying on my instincts, I knew:

I was in danger.

It didn't surprise me. What surprised me was how long it had taken. The moment I accepted the warden's offer to work the ADA yard with serial killers—men the general population wanted dead—I'd risked being green-lighted.

Now the order had finally come down. Somewhere, a high-ranking gang member had taken it to *La Mesa*, the Table, the ruling council. And they'd put me in the hat—the hit list.

When the yard officer stopped at my cell that morning, cuffs in hand, he asked, "Cuffs, Noguera?"

I met his eyes, thinking about throwing caution aside, but shook my head. "No, boss. I'm not going out."

Three days later, Joker stopped at my cell. We'd known each other thirty-six years, both arriving on San Quentin's death row as young men. Six-two, 224 pounds of muscle and violence.

"You made the right choice staying in," he said. "It's not personal, just business." He smiled, but his eyes were flat.

I stepped closer to the bars. "Then you won't take it personal when I punch your ticket at the gates of hell. Just business."

We locked eyes for a long moment. The air between us was thick, two predators measuring whether this was the day one of us would make the first move.

"You take care, Mr. Noguera," he said.

"You too, Ruben."

Later that morning, I was moved to the Administrative Segregation Unit—ASU, the hole—to await transfer. Because my death sentence had been reduced, the system treated me as if I were a new arrival. But San Quentin's mainline was only medium security, and death row inmates couldn't be placed there. Until my file was reviewed, I had to remain in the hole.

What should have been weeks turned into half a year in a four-by-nine-foot cage. A cold shower now and then. An hour, three times a week, in another cage outside. Word had traveled fast: I was a marked man. A green light followed me everywhere.

But this time, I carried it differently. I was marked not for betrayal or politics, but for something righteous—for doing everything I could to bring closure to the families of Naso's victims. That purpose steadied me.

My final conversation with him had come a few days before. I didn't know it would be the last time I spoke to him—or the last time I set foot on the yard. After all the years, all the maneuvering, he spoke not of murder or secrets but of football. That was it. A lifetime of violence behind him, and the parting words we shared were about a game.

On July 5, 2023, at 2:05 a.m., the transport team came.

"Noguera?"

"I'm awake."

"Name and number."

"Noguera, William. D-77200."

"Prepare for transport."

"Where to?"

"Is that your only box?"

"It is. I travel light."

They cuffed me and led me to Receiving and Release. Photographed. Loaded onto the bus. Through the gates, onto the road.

At the stoplight outside San Quentin, I cast one last glance at the stone walls, my home for nearly four decades. The towers rose like sentinels in the night, the same ones that had watched over me for most of my life.

"I beat you," I whispered. Then I faced forward. The light changed. I drew a deep breath and smiled.

I didn't look back.

38

Corcoran

During the transfer, I was carsick the entire ride—not being in a vehicle for more than thirty years had left me unprepared. By the time we pulled up to Corcoran, my stomach churned and my head pounded.

Two surprises waited for me.

The first came the moment I saw the prison itself. I had left one war zone only to enter another. Corcoran carried a deadly reputation for violence, gangs, and the infamous "gladiator pits," where guards staged inmate fights, sometimes to the death. Many men had died in those pits, and now I was headed for its most notorious unit: 4B, the 180s.

Each half-circle building had two concrete yards walled in by fifteen-foot barriers topped with razor wire, a gunner's post high above—perfect sight lines for officers who once bet on blood. It reminded me of the movie *Felon*. Standing there, I felt as if I'd stepped onto a set built for violence.

The second surprise came in Receiving and Release. Shackled, mask on, I radiated the same signal I had for decades: *dangerous*. Just as I was about to be placed in a holding cage, a voice called out.

"Noguera, hold up."

I turned to see a lieutenant I recognized.

"Lieutenant."

"Didn't expect to ever see you here, but I heard on the radio you were coming." He smiled. "Back in the day Ol' Willie would've loved to have you in his pit."

I let the weight of my eyes fall on him. "I'm not fighting for anyone, LT. Try me and you won't like the results."

He caught the meaning instantly and raised his hands. "My apologies, Noguera. It's not like that anymore. Things have changed—this is a program facility now. Rehabilitation, not violence."

I stayed quiet, skeptical, until he walked me through processing, had the chains and irons removed, and said, "Play your cards right, and you'll never wear cuffs again."

He was right. When we stepped onto the 4B yard, I entered a world I barely recognized. Several acres of grass stretched in front of me, with a track running around the perimeter. Men played volleyball, basketball, football, even strummed guitars or walked to classrooms. For the first time in four decades, I saw no gunners in towers. What stunned me most wasn't what I saw—it was what I didn't. Tension. On every yard I'd lived, it coiled tight, ready to explode. Here, it was gone.

Inside my new housing unit, I found more shocks. Men sat in theater-style seats watching a flat-screen TV. A microwave and ironing board sat nearby. My instinct immediately pictured the iron swung as a weapon, but no one seemed to think that way. Black, white, and brown sat side by side sharing food. Others listened to music through earbuds or tapped away on their tablets.

That's when a Mexican man approached.

"You William? Just come off death row?"

I locked in, my posture shifting, danger flashing in my eyes. "Who the fuck are you?"

He startled, then held up his hands. "I meant no disrespect, bro. I just wanted to welcome you. You're assigned to my cell."

I studied him before shaking his hand. "Yeah, I'm William. What's your name?"

"Reyes." He hesitated. "Are you going to stay?"

It was only at that moment I realized the others were watching. They weren't interested in him. They were interested in me. Was I a threat? The real question behind "Are you staying?" was whether I was an active gang member ready to shed blood to earn transfer.

"I'm staying."

And just like that, the tension eased. Men turned back to their business.

I didn't sleep the first few nights. After decades in a single cell, sharing space with anyone was disorienting. But I adjusted. I had to. I was serving life now, and there were no other options.

Within a month I was issued an Android tablet—another shock after decades of stone and steel. I could text, video call, even stream. That small screen was a game changer.

One of my first calls was to Jason Wolf of Fireside Pictures. Ken Mains and I had been working together on other unsolved murders tied to Joseph Naso, and Jason wanted to explore whether the decade of notes I'd kept could be developed into a series. From our first conversation, he and I clicked. We spent months poring over my notes and manuscript—the bones of this book. Soon Dick Wolf had signed on as executive producer, Peacock came aboard as the network, and law enforcement agencies began contacting me about the information I'd drawn from Naso. For the first time, I believed my work could bring families the closure they deserved.

Life at Corcoran steadied. I threw myself into self-help groups—anger management, domestic violence, criminal thinking. I founded Youth Core, a program to steer at-risk kids away from gangs, drugs, and the cycle of trauma that had shaped my life. I wanted to make a difference, inside and out.

Nearly a year in, I received a letter from my attorney. Andrew asked me to call. I didn't think much of it—after decades of appeals and hearings, I'd learned not to expect good news.

When I did call, Andrew hesitated before speaking.

"William, the judge wants to see you. He's tipping his hand. The DA has conceded that the special circumstances were bogus, and the judge is going to strike them. He'll reduce your sentence to twenty-five to life."

He went on to explain what he meant. He had asked the court to invoke Penal Code 1385, a California law that gives judges the authority to dismiss punishments they consider frivolous. In his brief, he laid out how much criminal law had changed since 1983: how the brain of an eighteen-year-old—the age I was when I committed murder—is now recognized as undeveloped; how the trauma of my upbringing had never been considered; how my trial attorney failed me; and how the "special circumstances" used to send me to death row—that I killed for financial gain—were built on coerced testimony.

The case had been botched from the beginning. And now, for the first time, a judge was ready to say it. I couldn't believe what I was hearing. The truth had broken through, and for the first time in forty-two years, I saw the light at the end of the tunnel.

On April 8, 2024, Superior Court Judge Lance Jensen followed through. He reduced my sentence to twenty-five to life, making me immediately eligible for parole, and ordered his findings sent to the board.

Three weeks later, a forensic psychologist rated me "moderate low" risk to ever reoffend. On January 28, 2025, the commissioners voted unanimously to grant me parole.

Forty-two years. Four decades of cages, chains, and killers. And yet I walked into Corcoran with a different purpose than when I entered San Quentin as a teenager. The years had scarred me, but they had also honed me.

I was alive. I had a voice. And I still had unfinished business.

The families of Joseph Naso's victims deserved the truth. I had promised them finality, no matter the cost. My freedom only sharpened that obligation.

What came next began with the cold cases still waiting in the dark.

39

Answers at Last

Counting down the days to my release, I spent as much time as possible supporting the investigations into Joseph Naso's unsolved murders. What had started as scraps of notes and hard-won conversations with Naso on San Quentin's death row was now drawing national attention. Peacock signed on to produce a four-part docuseries about what I had uncovered.

To prepare materials for the project, Ken Mains and producer Jason Wolf combed through old evidence lists and photographs. Buried in the paperwork, they found something extraordinary: twenty-six gold coins cataloged among the items seized from Naso's house. At first glance it was just property, but the number was unmistakable. Twenty-six coins. Twenty-six victims. Another of Naso's obsessions hiding in plain sight.

Detectives from Daly City, Berkeley, and Las Vegas—even the FBI—came to speak with me about the decade I had spent pulling confessions out of Naso. Many confirmed what I already knew: the patterns, the logic, the way his reasoning fit the murders. Several told me their agencies would be reopening cases, contacting families, and re-examining evidence in light of what I had gathered. That had been my goal all along. Not leverage for myself. Not bargaining power in court. But truth—for the victims, both known and unknown.

It would have been easy to make this about me. I was facing death when I first started, and there were ways to use what I uncovered to my advantage. But I never did. Not when a judge reconsidered my case. Not when the parole board weighed my future. I let them rule on the merits alone. Because for me, it has always been about the victims and their families. Integrity still mattered more than anything else.

Lynn Ruth Connes: The Girl from Berkeley

After the case reopened, Mains met with Lynn's younger brother, Lee Connes, now sixty-four, who manages the cemetery where their family is buried. After seeing Naso's confession and the supporting evidence, Lee said he was "99.9 percent sure" Naso killed his sister.

"It's amazing that after so many years, someone cared enough to try to solve it," he said. "We're lucky that Noguera was willing to get the ball rolling and cared enough to find out what happened."

Lynn Ruth Connes.

Lee is now considering updating his sister's memorial to reflect that she is no longer missing. "We were very close," he told Mains. "It's been so hard to ever say she was deceased. It takes a bit to settle in."

Meanwhile, investigators moved forward. Mains told Berkeley Police that he had solved their case, and by late 2024 he was also in touch with FBI Special Agent Martha Parker from the San Francisco field office. Parker told him she had been looking into Naso for the past year on the Connes case alongside Berkeley Police.

The FBI would not officially confirm the investigation. A public information officer replied only that "per longstanding policy, the FBI cannot confirm or deny the existence of an investigation." Berkeley Police were more direct: Officer Jessica Perry confirmed in an email that the department "is currently investigating this case and cannot comment on ongoing investigations," adding that they would issue a public statement once the work was complete.

Charlotte Cook: The Girl from Miami, Down Peninsula

Naso told me about every woman on his list except one: "Girl from Miami near down peninsula." Whenever I asked about her, he stiffened. "I don't want to talk about her right now," he'd say. "She's very personal." Each time I sensed he might go further, he pulled away, leaving me with scraps.

By then, Mains and I were already working side by side to solve the rest of Naso's List of Ten, along with the sixteen murders he claimed beyond it. I shared my few notes on the girl from Miami with Mains, and we went over them dozens of times—by phone, by text. Each time, we chased a lead into a dead end. Rabbit holes and nothing more.

Finally, Mains suggested we strip it all back and start fresh. Forget everything we had speculated, and focus only on what we knew for certain.

1. She existed. Every entry on the list corresponded to a real victim.
2. She had been visiting her sister in San Francisco.
3. She wasn't from Miami, Florida. For years, law enforcement assumed she was. It seemed obvious. But Naso had told me directly that she wasn't.
4. Naso hinted more than once that Caryl Chessman, his idol, "would approve."

That's where we began again.

From this standpoint, the work felt overwhelming. Searching through decades of missing and murdered women in the Bay Area meant looking backward from the 2000s into the '90s, '80s, and '70s with no name, no date, and nothing but the word "Miami" to guide us. An endless task.

Each file was another reminder of how many families had asked the same questions for years: "What happened to our daughter? And why?" That weight pressed on us every time we hit another dead end.

Mains had spent months combing through reports of young women who had disappeared in the 1970s but kept coming up empty-handed. But then, he cross-checked news reports of murders in the Oakland area, where Naso had maintained a one-room studio. Mains found several articles about a woman named Charlotte Cook. One had appeared in a local paper called the *Peninsula News*. The article described how Cook had been wearing an expensive camel hair coat the night she was killed.

DC Victim Identified

The body of a young woman found dumped at the base of the cliff at Thornton Beach in Daly City last Friday has been identified as that of Charlotte Cook, 19, of Oakland.

Coroner's Investigator Steve Hortin said the identification was made by the strangled girl's father, Neal Davis, of San Francisco. Davis was contacted by an aunt who read a newspaper description of the expensive camel's hair coat the girl was wearing and informed the father.

Hortin said the girl had been last reported alive Thursday afternoon when she left her Oakland home to visit a sister in San Francisco.

The coroner's investigator said that Mrs. Cook was a widow, her husband having been killed about 18 months ago in an Oakland halfway house, according to authorities in that city.

Report of Charlotte Cook's death.

When I read that line, my mind flashed back to one of my conversations with Naso. Almost offhand, he had told me the girl from Miami was wearing a "kick-ass jacket." I hadn't written it down at the time. Talking to him was like trying to hold water in my hands—every detail threatened to slip away before I could return to my cell and capture it. But paired with the article, the memory came roaring back as confirmation.

Charlotte Cook.

The victim had been found in Daly City—known locally as the "Gateway to the Peninsula." To Bay Area residents, the stretch below San Francisco has always been called simply the Peninsula, and Daly City sits right at its northern edge. Naso's phrase "near down peninsula" could easily have referred to that exact area. Charlotte Cook's body was discovered there at Thornton Beach, dumped over an embankment. She had been strangled with a brown belt, a crude but unmistakable signature of control.

The date was January 2, 1974—just days before Naso's birthday on January 7. I already knew he liked to give himself "a treat" around that time of year, as he had with Roxanne Roggasch.

Her name was Charlotte Cook.

The initials—C. C.—matched Naso's twisted tribute to Caryl Chessman. What were the odds?

Then came another piece that explained why Naso had been so reluctant to speak of her. Charlotte Cook was Black. From the standpoint of a death row inmate, that silence made perfect sense. In prison, especially in San Quentin, race is a razor's edge. Had the Black convicts learned Naso had raped and murdered a Black woman—a "sister"—he would have been held accountable. Stabbed, killed, or worse. He had seen it play out on the yard. That fear kept him quiet.

There was still the unanswered question about Miami. It obviously meant something important enough for Naso to write it on his list. But what? The answer came a couple of days later when Mains was studying a map of Oakland and noticed Miami Court, a tiny cul-de-sac north of MacArthur Boulevard, where Naso had his studio.

Miami Court: a cul-de-sac north of MacArthur Boulevard.

Armed with this information, Mains contacted the Daly City Police Department and shared the details of what we'd discovered. A couple of weeks later, Detective William Reininger and his partner from Daly City Homicide came to Corcoran prison to meet with me. I laid out everything—what Naso had said, what I suspected, and what I'd recorded in my notes over the years. By the end of our meeting, they were convinced that Charlotte Cook was the "Girl from Miami, near down peninsula." A cold case, unsolved for fifty years, finally had an answer.

Over the next few weeks, Mains met with Charlotte's family. It was difficult. We had reopened a wound that had never truly healed. By naming her, we made it real again. The emotions ran raw—grief, anger, sorrow—but also gratitude. At last, after half a century, they had some measure of closure.

The riddle of the "Girl from Miami" was solved. But for her family, it was never just a riddle. It was a mother, a daughter, a sister—a life stolen far too soon.

Rebecca Jean Dunn: The Girl from Las Vegas

You've already met Rebecca, the prostitute in Las Vegas. Naso took her to his studio near the Strip, strangled her, and left her body in the desert. Blond, round face, green eyes. Her name, he said, was Becca—short for Rebecca. She wasn't one of the women on the List of Ten, but part of the larger count of twenty-six victims he claimed.

For years, that was all I had: the story as Naso told it and the memory of her name. Then Mains gave her a history. Using facial recognition software, he matched one of the photographs from Naso's collage—the same collection of images Naso once handed me on death row—to a missing woman not on the list: Rebecca Jean Dunn.

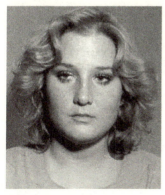

According to the Las Vegas Metropolitan Police Department, she was twenty-one, originally from San Diego. She was last seen on May 10, 1979.

At the time, Naso was living in Las Vegas, separated from his wife, and using a small studio near the Strip as his hunting ground. He even had the *Professional Photographer* article in hand—a prop he bragged about and used to disarm Rebecca the night he killed her.

Rebecca Jean Dunn.

The more I compared his description to Rebecca Dunn's photographs and the official record, the more it fit. Blond. Round face. Green eyes. A young woman whose trail ended abruptly that spring.

After Mains submitted his report, the Las Vegas Metropolitan Police

Department reopened Dunn's case. A source close to the investigation confirmed the review, though officials later stated publicly that no new leads had been developed. Rebecca remains officially a missing person, her body never recovered.

This wasn't a case we could hand back to a family with finality like Charlotte Cook's. But her name matters. It gives weight to what might otherwise have been another of Naso's faceless victims, discarded in the desert.

Rebecca Dunn was not just an entry in his hidden count of twenty-six. She was a daughter, a young woman with a life ahead of her. And she was more than "the girl from Las Vegas."

Pamela Lambson: The Second Girl on Mount Tam

We began on Mount Tam looking for one victim. Instead, the search uncovered the truth about another.

We had most of the details about the girl Naso first mentioned on Mount Tam, along with a map I'd drawn from those conversations, so Mains and I agreed we should start there. After contacting law enforcement, a search was organized. Dogs were deployed across the area—just as Naso had described. He had given me exact directions years earlier, step by step:

- Follow Highway 101 to Highway 1, then turn east near Stinson Beach.
- Take Panorama Highway as it curves north into Mount Tamalpais State Park.
- Turn left on Pantoll Road.
- Turn right onto Ridgecrest Boulevard and follow it north.
- Shortly before West Peak, veer off onto a narrow dirt road.
- Stop just past a dense cluster of trees above a meadow and the Arturo Trail.

That was where he said he left Leslie.

Law enforcement search for the "girl on Mt. Tam."

But they didn't find her.

Fifty years had passed since May 10, 1975, when Naso said he strangled her and dumped her in a ravine. Time, weather, and animals would have erased nearly everything.

Before the search began, investigators combed through records to see if any unidentified remains had been found on Mount Tam. That's when we learned another young woman had been discovered there in 1977. Her case had gone cold for more than thirty years, but she did have a suspect: Rodney Alcala, the Dating Game Killer.

In 2011, the Marin County Sheriff's Office held a press conference announcing they were "confident" Alcala had murdered nineteen-year-old Pamela Jean Lambson. Alcala was already on death row at San Quentin, and the fit seemed convenient: a notorious killer with a long record of rape and murder, a man the public already feared.

Part of the case against him rested on a single witness statement from 1977. The witness recalled seeing a man with dark hair past his collar speaking to Pamela at a clothing store on Fisherman's Wharf the day she vanished. Alcala did wear his hair that way at the time, but the witness never identified him directly, nor did the report describe the encounter as aggressive—only that the man spoke with her.

In the late 1970s, long hair on men was common. Dozens could have fit the description on any given day at the Wharf. Thin evidence, but it was enough for investigators to pin suspicion on Alcala and let the shadow follow him for decades.

But a closer look at the circumstances of Pamela's disappearance pointed elsewhere. She was an aspiring singer and actor, the kind of  young woman easily lured by promises of a camera and a career. She vanished after meeting a photographer who spotted her at an Oakland A's game, told her she was beautiful, and offered to help her with headshots. The next day, police found her battered body on Mount Tamalpais, posed near a trail.

That was Naso's signature. He had told me more than once that he hunted at A's games using his fake press passes and business cards. Posing victims was

Pamela Lambson.

also his hallmark. Alcala didn't pose women, and by most accounts, he wasn't even in Oakland at the time.

When I compared what Naso had said with the Lambson case file, the pieces fit:

- A young woman picked up at an Oakland A's game.
- Talk of modeling and photographs.
- Fisherman's Wharf as the meeting point.
- The body left on Mount Tam.
- Naso's own admission: "They blamed Alcala for one of my kills."

After I shared these details with Mains, along with the conversation I'd had with Alcala denying his involvement, he reviewed the case and agreed with me: Naso, not Alcala, was Pamela's killer. In 2024, Mains sent his full notes to the Marin County Sheriff's Office. For months there was no response. When pressed later, a department spokesperson confirmed that the cold-case team is now reviewing whether Naso had "any potential involvement" in Pamela's murder—but said there were no announcements scheduled.

The official story had never rung true for Pamela's family. Her brother, Michael Lambson, recalled warning her about trusting a stranger before she left to meet the photographer at Fisherman's Wharf. Pamela brushed it off. "He could be my dad, Mike," she said. At the time of her disappearance, Alcala was in his early thirties—smooth, attractive, younger than Pamela's father. Naso was a decade older, closer in age to her dad. The description fit him far better than it ever did Alcala.

Today, Michael and his brothers are convinced Naso was the real killer.

In the end, it wasn't Rodney Alcala's crime. It was Joseph Naso's.

Pamela Lambson was not just "the second girl on Mount Tam." She was nineteen years old, an aspiring performer, and one more victim hidden behind the mask of a different monster.

Together, the cases of Lynn Ruth Connes, Charlotte Cook, Rebecca Dunn, and Pamela Lambson showed what could be done with persistence, with listening, and with refusing to let the fragments slip away. Not every victim on Naso's list has been found, and many families are still waiting for answers. But for these four women, the silence was broken, their names spoken again, their stories set straight.

For me, it wasn't just about exposing Joseph Naso. It was about the women he tried to erase. Each one deserved to be remembered.

My time with Naso ended, but the work did not. As I prepared to leave prison behind, I knew the investigations would follow me into the free world. Law enforcement now saw me as more than an inmate on death row—I had become a witness, a collaborator, and a man determined to keep shining light into the darkest corners.

Epilogue

After forty-two years behind bars, I am finally free.

The steel and concrete cage that was once my world has crumbled behind me. I have walked away from it—not broken, not bitter, but forged into something new.

The boy who entered hell at eighteen is gone. In his place stands a man: older, reflective, alive with purpose. Prison didn't just confine me; it shaped me. It taught me to value the smallest freedoms: the sun on my face, the wind on my back, the simple joy of walking without a wall to stop me. I can run now. I can ride a bike. I can choose my path.

The world has changed since I last walked free. Or perhaps more accurately, I have changed. My lens, once filtered by survival and darkness, is now sharper, focused on what matters. And yet, even with this freedom, I remain tethered to the shadows—not as a prisoner but as a witness.

I've lived where monsters dwell. I've studied their behavior, gained their trust, and dragged their secrets into the light. That work is not over. It's only beginning.

Joseph Naso, the Portrait Killer, is still alive at ninety-one—proof that sometimes monsters endure longer than the lives they destroy. Ending his silence was never about ending him. What mattered were the women he cast aside, and the families who had waited decades for the truth.

Because out here—in the world you live in—those same monsters move among us, disguised by ordinary lives. Many turn away from that truth. I cannot. I won't. I know too much.

I am William A. Noguera. I walk free not just to live, but to serve.

I speak for the silenced.

I fight for the forgotten.

I write for the truth.

Through the Lens of a Monster is only the beginning. There are more stories to tell, more secrets to expose, more justice to deliver. My next chapter begins now, and you're invited to come with me.

Let's shine a light where others fear to look.

Acknowledgments

Through the Lens of a Monster is the product of more than a decade of dangerous, deep-cover investigative work. It exists because of one man's determination to bring truth and closure to the families of Joseph Naso's victims.

Writing this book was never just an act of storytelling. It was a commitment to uncovering the truth, no matter the cost—to pulling back the masks of killers and educating the public about the motives, desires, and logic behind serial murder.

I am deeply grateful to my publisher and editor, Sandra Jonas, who saw the potential in this project from the beginning. She took a chance on me when I was still behind bars on death row with no hope of release. Her vision, patience, and relentless belief in this story made this book possible.

To Detective Ken Mains: thank you for not turning away when I reached out. Your guidance, insight, and collaboration were instrumental in piecing together the fragments of a decades-long nightmare and helping to identify forgotten victims.

To Jason Wolf and Patrick DeLuca of Fireside Pictures: your faith in me and in the story I uncovered never wavered. Thank you for believing in my word and for transforming this investigation into a groundbreaking television series that gives voice to the silenced.

To my friends, Andy and Cindy Alas: you never let me give up.

Your encouragement grounded me through the darkest hours. Thank you for reading draft after draft, for your unshakable support, and for believing in the mission even when I doubted myself.

And finally, to the families of the victims—this book is for you. From the beginning, you were the reason I undertook this journey. Your pain, your loss, and your strength were never far from my mind. Seeking justice and closure for you kept me moving forward, even when my own life was at risk.

About the Author

WILLIAM A. NOGUERA is a pioneering expert on serial killers with a unique perspective, having spent forty-two years on San Quentin's death row before his release in 2025. He is also an internationally acclaimed artist whose work has been exhibited worldwide, and his insights into the criminal mind inspired the Oxygen True Crime docuseries *Death Row Confidential*, produced by Dick Wolf, Vanity Fair Studios, and Universal Television. His story has been featured in *Forbes*, the *New York Times*, the *San Francisco Chronicle*, and the *Guardian*.

Today, Noguera writes, speaks, and collaborates with law enforcement to expose the truth about the predators among us. When he isn't working, he can often be found on his Harley-Davidson—Scarlett.

Website: WilliamNoguera.com
Instagram: @DeadBodySociety
YouTube: @DeadBodySociety
TikTok: @Dead.Body.Society

28068231R00135